THE LEAST

SHALL BE THE

GREATEST

God's illuminated path

i

By D.R. Wasson Sr. © copyright 2017

Table of contents

Throughout the history of mankind, there have been those that stand out like lights that illuminate the pathway. Their lives were spent in peculiar ways that have shown the boundaries between righteous behavior and despotism. In the scope of all of the darkness that envelopes the world, God has set his peculiar people as guides to show the straight path to life. Never was it easy or without danger and was always a sacrifice of personal welfare. Without their sacrifices, the world might be much darker and evil would rule in a much more vicious way. It is easy for all of us to step behind our curtain of comfort and watch as someone else takes the heat. We all have our own lives to worry about and we tend to find a spot to relax and spend our days taking advantage of that which has been afforded us. There is a force of evil in this world that is trying to dominate and bring destruction to the souls of people. When someone rises up to put down the evil they are met with great opposition from the darkness. Perseverance and great faith in God give supernatural strength to become one of those beaming lights that keep the boundaries from being breached. God's word is like a video tape of some of these great ones that have their beginnings in less than humble ranks. Their stories give us an example of selfless trust in the only one that can make a difference in the world for the healing of the nations. The center of it all is the greatest sacrifice of all time that was given by

God Himself for the redeeming of life and the light of people.

Mar 10:42-45 KJV But Jesus called them to him, and saith unto them, Ye know that they which are accounted to rule over the Gentiles exercise lordship over them; and their great ones exercise authority upon them. (43) But so shall it not be among you: but whosoever will be great among you, shall be your minister: (44) And whosoever of you will be the chiefest, shall be servant of all. (45) For even the Son of man came not to be ministered unto, but to minister, and to give his life a ransom for many.

Jesus is the bonfire in which everyone that is willing, can light their torch for the journey through the darkness of an evil world. The humility of someone that doesn't qualify according to the world's standards is the very fuel that burns the brightest in the kingdom of God.

Noah

The world had seen darkness, but as the population began to increase there were more and more ways to express evil and complete rebellious behavior. There came a time when even some of the angels from heaven had integrated into the population and began to teach people more heinous and evil ways that were destructive, that perverted life and the flesh. They were teaching more efficient ways to commit murder and to make killing a way of life as violence had begun to fill the earth. They taught sexual perversions and evil ways to exploit unnatural desires. These angels were the watchers that were appointed to keep order from the spirit realm that mankind may find their way to a prosperous increase of humanity and to fulfill God's command to multiply and replenish the earth. Angels were always supposed to minister to the wayward and help them back to their purpose to subdue the earth. These watchers had so corrupted the human race because of their having procreated with human women that there was no more hope left for them. The offspring of these angels and women were giants and these giants were evil to the core. The whole earth was filled with creatures that were not made by God but were hideous monstrosities devised at the hands of the watchers. Mankind had fallen deep into the abyss of deception and was worshiping the darkness of these perverted life forms. They were assimilating into each other to make a mixture of hybrid human beings that were not made in the image of God. Because of the fall of man and the propensity to sin, the watchers only succeeded in bringing about the destruction of the planet and the people that populated it.

There was one however that was not moved by fear and had his faith in God the Creator of the universe. In the midst of terror and obscene violence within the darkness of a sinful world; he remained a light. His name was called Noah which means "to rest". When we see the evil that permeates our society and have to battle against its advancement; it sometimes makes one feel weary inside. Every day there is something that takes place in the world that makes it very clear that evil is alive and well in the earth today. Injustice and unnecessary death and destruction remind us of the need for vigilance in this life. Noah stood against impossible odds and yet he kept his heart from evil. He was a preacher of righteousness in the midst of the multitudes of those that were teaching lies. His light shined in a dark and oppressive environment and he spoke the truth. One day he was given the word from God that the end of humanity was coming. Now he had to warn the world that they were in imminent danger of destruction.

Gen 6:5-8 KJV And GOD saw that the wickedness of man was great in the earth, and that every imagination of the thoughts of his heart was only evil continually. (6) And it repented the LORD that he had made man on the earth, and it grieved him at his heart. (7) And the LORD said, I will destroy man whom I have created from the face of the earth; both man, and beast, and the creeping thing, and the fowls of the air; for it repenteth me that I have made them. (8) But Noah found grace in the eyes of the LORD.

This destruction would come in the form of a flood over the whole world. Even today as we teach about this worldwide flood; there are those that will speak evil of this truth and make a mockery of it. We must stand for God's truth against all comers that would pervert that truth, as did Noah; his words were true even though his peers would not believe. Those that were close to him did believe and were on his side. He was instructed to build an ark; a giant boat in the middle of the dry land. He probably became the brunt of every joke and the center of ridicule. How many of us could endure that kind of persecution and stay the course without quitting? Faith was his life preserver in a sea of doubt and unbelief amidst the crashing waves of foul words and destructive attacks. Mental abuse is difficult to endure unless you are shielded by faith and trust in God.

Eph 6:13-17 KJV Wherefore take unto you the whole armour of God, that ye may be able to withstand in the evil day, and having done all, to stand. (14) Stand therefore, having your loins girt about with truth, and having on the breastplate of righteousness; (15) And your feet shod with the preparation of the gospel of peace; (16) Above all, taking the shield of faith, wherewith ye shall be able to quench all the fiery darts of the wicked. (17) And take the helmet of salvation, and the sword of the Spirit, which is the word of God:

Noah preached to a violent crowd of dark spiritual wickedness, and he shined his light out to them even though they hated him. None of them will have an excuse in the day of judgment when they stand before the Ancient of Days because they were warned by Noah. He was not a lunatic as he was probably labeled in his day, but preached what God had said.

Gen 6:11-13 KJV The earth also was corrupt before God, and the earth was filled with violence. (12) And God looked upon the earth, and, behold, it was corrupt; for all flesh had corrupted his way upon the earth. (13) And God said unto Noah, The end of all flesh is come before me; for the earth is filled with violence through them; and, behold, I will destroy them with the earth.

He believed God's word even when it looked impossible. Consider that giant boat in the middle of a dry land and how ridiculous it must have seemed to the skeptical mind. Sometimes when we are called, to tell the truth of God's miraculous power we are confronted with what may seem to be impossible odds. We speak today of the return of Christ for His people but are met with skeptical rhetoric from many sources even Christians. We have to stand like Noah against the pressures of unbelief and doubt, so with faith, we stand.

Now there came a day of reckoning when God would begin to fulfill His word to Noah. I can't imagine what must have taken place when God told Noah to fill the ark with the animals. People must have looked on with amazement at the tremendous faith that Noah had shown by leading animals into the wooden monstrosity that stood out as an enormous monument to their ridicule.

Gen 6:17-19 KJV And, behold, I, even I, do bring a flood of waters upon the earth, to destroy all flesh, wherein is the breath of life, from under heaven; and every thing that is in the earth shall die. (18) But with thee will I establish my covenant; and thou shalt come into the ark, thou, and thy sons, and thy wife, and thy sons' wives with thee. (19) And of every living thing of all flesh, two of every sort shalt thou bring into the ark, to keep them alive with thee; they shall be male and female.

The door was shut behind them as onlookers gazed at what they saw as a crazy man and his display of mindless fantasy. But the clouds soon moved in and the first drop of rain ever fell and soon was joined by more and more raindrops until it became a deluge. The earth parted and there were great fountains of gushing water from the ground. Soon the people would have to seek higher ground. Now, what must have been their thoughts concerning the wild story that Noah had told them? It will be the same way when Christ returns in that He will come at a time when people don't expect. The people of Noah's day surely didn't believe that he was telling the truth and didn't bother to change their ways. They were living as if nothing would change, but it did and was too late for them to repent. Noah would soon become the father of all the living in that he was the Patriarch of all living human beings that would multiply. He also was the one that God used to save the animal kingdom and so his legacy will live forever. Noah was the least of the least because he was the focus of ridicule and resentment. In a world of conformity to the powers of darkness, Noah stayed his course in spite of popular consensus. He is a great light on that pathway and leaves us with a pattern of action that can show us the way to great things and a life that will be counted as a guiding light as well.

Dan 12:3 KJV And they that be wise shall shine as the brightness of the firmament; and they that turn many to righteousness as the stars for ever and ever.

Abraham

By the time that people had multiplied again on the face of the earth, there was a place called Ur of the Chaldeans. This was a place of idol worship where there were many gods in the form of statues and other objects that depicted false gods. Abram which means "exalted father" was living there among the polytheistic population. It is amazing how that people are so easily turned against the true and living God to dumb idols and fables that oppose God. Abram at that time had no children but his name would suggest otherwise. Even Abram's name carries hope in that he would one day see his name fulfilled. Among a culture of false god worship, Abram would hear God's voice and he would then be faced with a decision.

Gen 12:1-3 KJV Now the LORD had said unto Abram, Get thee out of thy country, and from thy kindred, and from thy father's house, unto a land that I will shew thee: (2) And I will make of thee a great nation, and I will bless thee, and make thy name great; and thou shalt be a blessing: (3) And I will bless them that bless thee, and curse him that curseth thee: and in thee shall all families of the earth be blessed.

Abram had much substance and his move would require great faith because he would have to leave his place of comfort to move to a place that he had never seen. As Noah believed God and built an ark, so Abram would have to believe God and move away from his home of seventy-five years. He would also be responsible for the welfare of all of his servants and livestock on the road to a place that he didn't know. Sometimes we may be asked to take a step in faith and do something of which we have no prior knowledge. You may have to believe God for something sometime and make a move or take on a responsibility that would be easier not to do. Abram was given a promise of a land and a people of his own. What would the elders have thought of Abram in his leaving on a promise of a God that the rest of them didn't know? Abram was the first of his people to become monotheistic and that would probably have gained him disrespect, as they had gods for many things. He would have to give up a place of prominence in the community and believe God for something greater. His nephew Lot followed him in his sudden change and must have had much respect for him to gather all that he had and to go into the unknown. With all of their substance, their servants and all of their livestock Abram and his nephew pull up stakes and leave their homeland. God was with Abram and he began to increase, he and Lot began to grow in substance as they traveled to the place where God would show Abram. They became too many to dwell together and so Abram gave the choice to Lot as to the land that he would dwell in. Lot chose the fertile land that was before them so Abram took his substance and turned to go another way. Abram had the right to choose first but he gave that choice to his nephew, and God was with Abram.

Gen 13:6-11 KJV And the land was not able to bear them, that they might dwell together: for their substance was great, so that they could not dwell together. (7) And there was a strife between the herdmen of Abram's cattle and the herdmen of Lot's cattle: and the Canaanite and the Perizzite dwelled then in the land. (8) And Abram said unto Lot, Let there be no strife, I pray thee, between me and thee, and between my herdmen and thy herdmen; for we be brethren. (9) Is not the whole land before thee? separate thyself, I pray thee, from me: if thou wilt take the left hand, then I will go to the right; or if thou depart to the right hand, then I will go to the left. (10) And Lot lifted up his eyes, and beheld all the plain of Jordan, that it was well watered every where, before the LORD destroyed Sodom and Gomorrah, even as the garden of the LORD, like the land of Egypt, as thou comest unto Zoar. (11) Then Lot chose him all the plain of Jordan; and Lot journeyed east: and they separated themselves the one from the other.

Abram sacrificed the greater for the least and he took that more difficult road so that Lot could dwell in a place that he felt would be good for himself. Abram kept increasing and God blessed him as He had promised. God has promised to each one of us that He will direct our paths if we trust Him.

Pro 3:5-6 KJV Trust in the LORD with all thine heart; and lean not unto thine own understanding. (6) In all thy ways acknowledge him, and he shall direct thy paths.

Believe these words as Abram believed and listen for the direction of God because as He was with Abram He will also be with you. Sometimes it may seem that He isn't there but trust Him anyway because He is one who keeps His promises. As the scripture says; "lean not to your own understanding, but in all your ways acknowledge Him" this is faith in what He said. The world has their way, but God has another way and that is the right way.

Rom 8:28 KJV And we know that all things work together for good to them that love God, to them who are the called according to his purpose.

As Abram reached the land that God had promised He visited him again and this time He expanded on His word by changing Abram's name to Abraham which means "father of multitudes". He also changed Abraham's wife's name from Sarai meaning "Princess", to Sarah that means " mother of nations". God told Abraham that He would give him a son. As of yet Abraham and Sarah were childless because Sarah was barren. This is an attribute of God in that He had pronounced the impossible to become the promise. Sarah could not have children, but God said that Abraham would be the father of a nation. Because Abraham was willing to believe God, he was the father of a people that God would choose for Himself to be His people. These would be the people that would carry the written word of God to the world. Abraham had a son by Hagar which was Sarah's handmaid, but this wasn't the son of the promise. God would give Sarah a son at the age of ninety. Again this is a promise based on the impossible, not only was Sarah barren, but she was long past the age to reproduce. Do you believe God for the impossible? Most readers of this story would think that it was a fable and not true. God has produced an entire nation of people through a ninety-year-old barren womb. Not only that, but He also brought His own Son through these miraculous people. Abraham had his struggles yet he believed God for the promise and although he didn't see the fulfillment of a nation in his lifetime, he did rejoice to see the fulfillment of the impossible that he had a son of promise. There is more in that He has seen the fulfillment of the nation and Messiah after his leaving this earth:

Joh 8:52-58 KJV Then said the Jews unto him, Now we know that thou hast a devil. Abraham is dead, and the prophets; and thou sayest, If a man keep my saying, he shall never taste of death. (53) Art thou greater than our father Abraham, which is dead? and the prophets are dead: whom makest thou thyself? (54) Jesus answered, If I honour myself, my honour is nothing: it is my Father that honoureth me; of whom ye say, that he is your God: (55) Yet ye have not known him; but I know him: and if I should say, I know him not, I shall be a liar like unto you: but I know him, and keep his saying. (56) Your father Abraham rejoiced to see my day: and he saw it, and was glad. (57) Then said the Jews unto him, Thou art not yet fifty years old, and hast thou seen Abraham? (58) Jesus said unto them, Verily, verily, I say unto you, Before Abraham was, I am.

Abraham has seen this day and rejoiced at it so he has seen the fulfillment of God's promise in every way. In some way maybe Jesus is saying that after the resurrection, Abraham has seen Him in the future, because He was before him, or perhaps Abraham had seen Him from paradise. None the less, Abraham has seen God's promise to him as God has kept His promise. Now it is up to you to believe God's promises and to live according to them even if you don't see them as yet. Believe without doubting because the world will disagree with you, but the wisdom of the world will have its end and be destroyed, but God's wisdom is eternal. Will you stand with faithful Abraham and be a light for God or will you go the way of the world because of what it may look like at the time? Abraham's faith transcended time and space and worked into the future and he became a great light on that pathway to God's perfect plan.

Jacob

Inside the womb of Rebekah, the wife of Abraham's son of the promise: Isaac, there were twins wrestling. This is significant because there would be yet another wrestling match in the future.

Gen 25:21-26 KJV And Isaac intreated the LORD for his wife, because she was barren: and the LORD was intreated of him, and Rebekah his wife conceived. (22) And the children struggled together within her; and she said, If it be so, why am I thus? And she went to enquire of the LORD. (23) And the LORD said unto her, Two nations are in thy womb, and two manner of people shall be separated from thy bowels; and the one people shall be stronger than the other people; and the elder shall serve the younger. (24) And when her days to be delivered were fulfilled, behold, there were twins in her womb. (25) And the first came out red, all over like an hairy garment; and they called his name Esau. (26) And after that came his brother out, and his hand took hold on Esau's heel; and his name was called Jacob: and Isaac was threescore years old when she bare them.

The true character of Jacob was signified by that fact that he grabbed the heel of his brother Esau. He so desired the prominence that even from the beginning he put forth the effort to take it. Esau would become the manly one that was a hunter and was hairy and according to his father, he smelled like the fields. Jacob was the plain one and dwelt in tents. As he grew up he was the lesser of the two in that he was not the firstborn. Jacob desired the birthright and it meant very much to him, more so than to his brother Esau. Esau was obviously Isaac's favorite, but Jacob was the one that God had chosen for the promise. The birthright was the double portion and the one that would carry on the household after the father. Jacob desired to be the one that would be that patriarch in his line after Isaac. The rule was that the birthright belonged to Esau and he was supposed to carry the name for Isaac. There was a promise made to Abraham the boy's grandfather and Jacob was not to be the heir of that promise. There was a time when Esau had been out hunting and was exhausted and hungry. Jacob had made some stew and Esau desired some of it, so this

Jacob saw as an opportunity. He told Esau that he would trade the stew for his birthright, and Esau agreed. Esau must not have had much regard for the birthright and lived only in the moment. The King James reads that Esau despised his birthright; the word despised means to esteem lightly. Even if Jacob couldn't apprehend the inheritance of Isaac, he could attain the promise of God and with his mother's help, he did just that. The time came when Isaac was near to his end in this life and he sent Esau out to hunt venison for him to eat, meanwhile, Rebekah had overheard what was happening. While Esau was gone Rebeckah hatched a plan to get Isaac to give the blessing to Jacob. The name Jacob means "supplanter" to trip up or overthrow. This is an expression of the nature of Jacob's quest for the birthright. We also have a birthright as when we were born again, we were given a birthright as children. How important is that birthright to you? We've been given a promise of inheritance in the kingdom along with Jacob. When we trusted Jesus Christ as Savior we were made children according to the promise.

Rom 8:16-17 KJV The Spirit itself beareth witness with our spirit, that we are the children of God: (17) And if children, then heirs; heirs of God, and joint-heirs with Christ; if so be that we suffer with him, that we may be also glorified together.

Gal 3:27-29 KJV For as many of you as have been baptized into Christ have put on Christ.

(28) There is neither Jew nor Greek, there is neither bond nor free, there is neither male nor female: for ye are all one in Christ Jesus. (29) And if ye be Christ's, then are ye Abraham's seed, and heirs according to the promise.

Some people don't understand what that means and they esteem lightly the promise of the inheritance as did Esau. This is the promise that Jacob was so intent on receiving that he was willing to deceive his father to get it. That is not righteous, but it is faith in the promise of God, and that is the thing that God can work with. Rebekah cloaked Jacob in goatskin and sent him into Isaac with a goat prepared for him to eat. She instructed him to say that he was Esau because Isaac's eyesight was very poor. Isaac felt the hairy goatskin and smelled the field on Jacob and believed him to be Esau and so he spoke the blessing over him. God would honor that blessing because of the faithfulness of Isaac and the power of words. Life and death are in the power of the tongue and on that day Isaac had spoken the life of a nation into Jacob. Jacob did diligently seek after the blessing of the Lord and proved his faith with his persistence. Maybe Esau didn't have much faith in God or maybe God held him to his word as trading his birthright for stew, but in the end, Esau lost that blessing. Jacob after what had been done had to flee for his life for fear that Esau would kill him.

Gen 27:41 KJV And Esau hated Jacob because of

the blessing wherewith his father blessed him: and Esau said in his heart, The days of mourning for my father are at hand; then will I slay my brother Jacob.

It's funny how that while Esau still had the blessing, he didn't give it much thought, but when he lost it, somehow now it becomes valuable to him. How many people in the church have that attitude today? Two hours on Sunday are plenty to last the week and God is not considered until He's needed. God desires for us to seek Him diligently every day and all day long. He desires to be prominent in our lives so that He can be our continual guide as He makes us into someone great as only He can do. Isaac upon hearing that Esau would kill Jacob, sent him to live with his uncle Laban and to marry into the family and not to take a wife of the Canaanites. On the way, Jacob found a place where he would sleep for the night and made a pillow with a stone and went to sleep. That night would be one to be remembered in that his quest for the blessing would be realized. As he fell asleep, he saw a ladder or could be translated as staircase, and angels ascending and descending on it. The Lord stood above it and spoke to him the blessing that he so fervently sought after. Jacob had received the birthright and now would be in the great line of the Patriarchs and his faith would be rewarded. When he woke in the morning, he set up the stone that was his pillow and poured oil on it and called the place Bethel. The meaning of the word is this in Hebrew: Beit meaning house and El meaning God thus he called it the house of God. You can see how that all of the spiritual blessings were highly adored by Jacob, even though he was not perfect, he did believe with his whole heart. This is a heart that moves God in that He is more important than life itself and is well worth pursuing.

Psa 42:1 KJV ... As the hart panteth after the water brooks, so panteth my soul after thee, O God.

When Jacob got to his destination he found the woman that he desired to be his bride, Rachel. His eye was for her only and again his determination and persistence would have to be his ministers through the ordeal that he would soon encounter. Jacob agreed to work seven years for the hand of Rachel and after the seven years had ended, it was time for the wedding ceremony. Laban made a big feast for Jacob and after they had celebrated into the night, Laban brought the bride to Jacob. I don't know if there was a lot of drinking or if it was too dark to see but in the morning Jacob found out that he was given Leah as his wife. Perhaps Jacob's willingness to deceive was a family trait and now he was reaping what he had sewn. This is proof that even when we have a heart for God and seek Him, it doesn't mean that we are exempt from the consequences of our actions. Jacob was again persistent in that he worked another seven years to have Rachel. Jacob had twelve sons and one daughter between the two wives that he had married. Now would come the time for Laban to reap the consequences of his actions against Jacob. Jacob's persistence would again pay off and he was blessed by God in all that he did. Jacob and Laban struck a deal in the which that all of the spotted and speckled livestock would go to Jacob for wages and all the normal unblemished would remain with Laban. So it was that when the animals mated, Jacob put sticks in the water that they drank and their offspring came out spotted and speckled. Also, he did the same when it came to the strong of the herds and the weak so that all of Laban's herds were of the weak being solid in color and the spotted were strong. Jacob became very wealthy and prominent and Laban was on the losing end. The Lord spoke again to Jacob and told him to return back to the land from which he came.

Gen 31:3 KJV And the LORD said unto Jacob, Return unto the land of thy fathers, and to thy kindred; and I will be with thee.

Jacob took all that he had and headed out leaving Laban scantly supplied with his solid colored livestock. As Jacob made his journey his faithfulness was again rewarded as a host of angels met him and he named the place Mahanaim, meaning "two camps". He there divided his camp into two and made a gift for Esau as he had heard that Esau was on his way to where he was and feared the worse. Jacob sent them all ahead and he stayed there and he wrestled there with an Angel until morning. He again was persistent in that he would not release the Angel until He blessed him. The Angel pulled his hip out of the socket and gave him his blessing changing his name to Israel.

Gen 32:28 KJV And he said, Thy name shall be called no more Jacob, but Israel: for as a prince hast thou power with God and with men, and hast prevailed.

Here we have yet another light on the pathway, rewarded to the faith and persistence of a man that sought the favor of God. This is a picture of the faith that it takes to see great things in this life and to know the power of the Creator in every situation that we face.

Joseph

Joseph was the favorite and everybody knew it, including Joseph. He was the son of Israel's old age and by that time perhaps Israel was more like a grandfather than a father to Joseph. This seems to be a common flaw among the family as Isaac favored Esau and now Jacob does the same in the case of Joseph. God had favored Jacob over Esau, not because He loved him more, but that Jacob valued God and His promise, where Esau did not. Jacob sought after God's favor but it wasn't very important to Esau. God is no respecter of persons and has no favorites, however, He shows favor when He's pleased and that comes from having faith in Him.

Heb 11:6 KJV But without faith it is impossible to please him: for he that cometh to God must believe that he is, and that he is a rewarder of them that diligently seek him.

Joseph might have been a little spoiled, but he did respect the promise of God and the birthright. He was given a robe it says of many colors which in the time period would have been very costly. I suppose that every time his brothers saw him, the coat would be like a neon sign, blasting in their faces that he was the favored son. There was more that had his brothers fuming as well and that was his dreams. Joseph was a dreamer and had a gift of interpretation as well. All of us have dreams, however not all of us give much time to them. God gives dreams so that we may find answers, but not everybody pays attention to them.

Job 33:14-16 KJV For God speaketh once, yea twice, yet man perceiveth it not. (15) In a dream, in a vision of the night, when deep sleep falleth upon men, in slumberings upon the bed; (16) Then he openeth the ears of men, and sealeth their instruction,

Dreams are spiritual pictures that have meaning in this physical world and it is up to the dreamer to learn the language. Dreams are symbolic for a reason and that is that we have to seek to find the meaning of them. God hides the meaning in symbols and we must seek His ways and His word to uncover His instruction.

Pro 25:2 KJV It is the glory of God to conceal a thing: but the honour of kings is to search out a matter.

Joseph; by applying himself to the dreams and their meanings shows that he was seeking God in his heart and the same goes for anyone of us even today. We don't know what goes on in the heart of someone else but God does and He rewards faithfulness. Perhaps the brothers were more interested in the things of the world to spend much time seeking God. They cared about the birthright, but did they care about the promise? The bible says that they hated Joseph, there was jealousy involved and they couldn't speak kindly to him. That is understandable under the circumstances, but that is the sin nature that hates. One day while tending the sheep, Joseph didn't know when to keep silent to his brothers and told them of a dream that he had with an obvious meaning. He told them that they were gathering wheat and his bundle stood up and theirs all came and bowed down to his. They really hated him now because his dream said that they would bow down to Joseph and that didn't go over well with them. This dream was a true word from God but knowing how much they hated him, he didn't show much discretion in telling them. It almost looks like Joseph used the dream as a way to get at them because they hated him. After a while, he dreamed again and told them that the sun, moon and eleven stars bowed down to him, that perhaps was the final straw with his brothers. He told his father Israel and he responded negatively as well because he insinuated that he and his mother would also bow to him. Jacob, however, held these dreams in regard in his heart, that maybe it was from God. Now we have a situation going on here, everyone is now apprehensive about the dreams, but God can use bad situations as well. Remember that the seeds that we sew will be the harvest that we reap. This is no different even though Joseph seeks the Lord; he also is sewing discord in his family by his boasting of his dreams. That doesn't mean that God can't use him, but He must bring about a change of heart. That would come soon, as his brothers were feeding the flocks at Shechem, his father sent him to see how things were going with them. That was probably not the wisest thing to do at the time but would be the turning point for Joseph's life. They had moved on to Dothan and Joseph had to chase them down. They saw him coming from far off and conspired to kill him, that's how much they hated him. Hate sometimes clouds wisdom and can have devastating effects if it's not checked. Ruben was the one that used at least some wisdom and suggested that they throw him into a pit. His plan was that he would return later to retrieve Joseph and bring him home again. They threw him into the pit and sat down to eat. About that time they saw a band of Ishmaelite merchants and rather than kill him, they sold him as a slave to these Nomads. When Ruben returned, he was angry that they had sold Joseph and he tore his clothes, so at least Ruben was merciful towards him even if only for his father's sake. Now they had to make up a story to tell their father what had happened to Joseph. They devised a plan and killed a goat and dipped the multicolored coat in the blood. They returned home and told Israel that they found the coat but not Joseph, so Israel concluded that Joseph had been eaten by wild animals. Now his heart was broken and all of the dreams that Joseph had told him would now seem to be just fantasy and depression would oppress him. The process now begins for Joseph as he would have to humble himself to stay alive. Life can change in a moment of time and everything that you are familiar with can become history. Joseph was now in a situation that he couldn't predict but he handled well all things that he encountered. It may have been that the dreams were a life preserver for him as he knew in his heart that they were true. He perhaps looked beyond his miserable situation and saw the final outcome that he would be one day exalted to a high position. If God tells you something that He will do then you have a promise to hold on to in the dark times in life.

Psa 119:105 KJV ...Thy word is a lamp unto my feet, and a light unto my path.

God's favor was on Joseph because the man that purchased him from the merchants eventually made him head over his household. He was wise and he had the blessing of the Lord, as his faith had proven. You may have to humble yourself at times, but there is always reward in Christ when you use wisdom. Joseph was a slave but he had favor with his master as God's word is always proven out in this life.

Pro 16:7 KJV When a man's ways please the LORD, he maketh even his enemies to be at peace with him.

Try to walk in the light of wisdom; always knowing that God is pleased with those that have faith in Him. Joseph's journey isn't over yet and he has much to learn before he reaches the place where God can use him in the greatest way. It is no mystery that when someone is walking in God's will and is blessed, that Satan has to try to destroy it. Joseph's test would come in the form of a woman; his master's wife and her desire to have him. Now I must say this that what was so appealing to the woman was the very thing that would keep her from him. If Joseph would have been willing to take her then he would no longer be the man that she desired. His integrity was the dominating attribute of his personality and that was the thing that kept him from giving in to her. His faith in God and reverence for Him would not allow him to bring harm to his master by sleeping with his wife. Most of all He would be in rebellion against God's law and he wanted no part of that. There came a day when Joseph entered the house and found no one there except his master's wife and she proceeded to entice him. He didn't comply but she grabbed his garment and he fled leaving his garment in her hand. She then called for the servants of the house and accused Joseph of attempted rape. You see how that an innocent person can be destroyed by deception. Satan is a deceiver from the beginning and he accuses God's people continually. Joseph was thrown into prison and now another test begins for him. He was innocent of any crime and maintained his integrity because God was with him even in the prison. He was eventually elevated to a position of authority within the ranks of the prisoners and was in charge of them. The keeper of the prison trusted Joseph because he was wise and again the fact that he had integrity. Can you be trusted no matter what the situation? Can God trust you even in the small things? When you are faithful in the small things, He will trust you with more. This is a lesson for all of us in that we must show integrity in menial tasks and then He will trust us in greater things. Remember that providence rules in the life of a believer and God is our guide. He will soon provide the opportunity for Joseph to make a connection with the future. The Pharaoh had become suspicious with his butler and his baker and had them put into prison. As providence would have it, they were put under Joseph's care. One morning as Joseph came to their ward he noticed that they were both bothered by something. Joseph inquired of them what was wrong and they each told him of a dream that they had the night before. Isn't God wonderful? Joseph was the only one that could tell them the meaning of their dreams and they just happened to be in the same place where he was. There is a purpose for everything to the believer and this for Joseph was the beginning of his journey out of that prison one day.

Rom 8:28 KJV And we know that all things work together for good to them that love God, to them who are the called according to his purpose.

Joseph told them what would befall them in the near future by the interpretation of their dreams. The baker did not fare well as his destination was the chopping block, but the butler got good news in that he would be restored to his position. Joseph told the butler to remember him when he got out. It came to pass as Joseph had said; the baker lost his head and the butler got his position back, but he forgot Joseph. Two years would pass before Joseph's journey would culminate into his final destination. Joseph suffered thirteen years with his dreams in his heart that he knew would one day become a reality. Just as his father Jacob was determined upon the promise, so Joseph was determined upon his dreams. They both trusted God in bad situations and faith carried them to victory. Even though Joseph became a slave and spent time in prison for a crime he didn't commit; he was faithful and never relented. Pharaoh had two dreams and was shaken about them. Again, providence would arise and the butler then remembered Joseph. This was the final rung on Joseph's ladder to his dreams and so he interpreted Pharaoh's dreams. Pharaoh was so impressed by Joseph that he made him second only to himself in authority in the whole empire. Joseph's dreams had come true and his family did come to bow before him in Egypt. After seven years of plenty there came seven years of drought and in those days, Joseph had his family moved into the land of Goshen in Egypt where they would survive the great drought. Joseph confronted his brothers but he had no hatred for them in what they did to him.

Gen 45:4-8 KJV And Joseph said unto his brethren, Come near to me, I pray you. And they came near. And he said, I am Joseph your brother, whom ye sold into Egypt. (5) Now therefore be not grieved, nor angry with yourselves, that ye sold me hither: for God did send me before you to preserve life. (6) For these two years hath the famine been in the land: and yet there are five years, in the which there shall neither be earing nor harvest. (7) And God sent me before you to preserve you a posterity in the earth, and to save your lives by a great deliverance. (8) So now it was not you that sent me hither, but God: and he hath made me a father to Pharaoh, and lord of all his house, and a ruler throughout all the land of Egypt.

This attitude of Joseph's was one of humility and wisdom and it is a quality of greatness. Here is yet another light on that pathway that shows us how an attitude can make all the difference to God in our lives. Always remember that God is in control and as we don't always know the purpose; we can rest assured that God has a place of our dreams in the end. When we walk the way of our faith we are trusting in God that guides our path as He did for Joseph.

Moses

There came a day when a new Pharaoh came to power that did not know Joseph. He saw how that the Hebrew people flourished in Goshen and it troubled him. Earlier Joseph had given the land of Goshen to his family, which was seventy people counting Joseph's sons and God blessed them. Now in the time of the new Pharaoh, there was an enormous population in the territory of the Hebrews. Joseph was gone and his legacy now was placed in the annals of history. Pharaoh was worried that if the Hebrew people were to rebel, that they were so many that they could join with neighboring nations and defeat Egypt in battle. This is how fear works in that it creates a bad situation that doesn't exist and will cause someone to act upon it. Fear will rule in the mind of the unbeliever because he has no solid foundation with which to anchor himself. Fear is the opposite of faith and it is destructive to the life of the one under its control. Pharaoh put the Hebrew people to task and assigned hard taskmasters to them and now they were slaves to Egypt. This was a dark time for the Hebrew people that lasted four hundred years. Many people were born as slaves and died as slaves in this terrible time in history. God blessed them even though they were in bondage as they were very fruitful in having children. Providence would once again intervene in a time of tragedy. Pharaoh gave a command that every son that was born to them was to be cast into the river and every daughter could live. There was a son born that was beautiful to look at and his mother hid him for three months. Afterward, she made a small boat out of bulrushes and set him in the river. It is ironic that the same river that was supposed to be his grave turned out to be his salvation. His sister was told to follow him and see where he ends up. As it happened, Pharaoh's daughter was bathing in the river just when the boat passed by. She saw the baby inside and loved him. Can you see the hand of God at work here? Sometimes we don't understand why things happen the way that they do, but when it comes to faith we know there is a greater purpose. God had not forgotten His people and He sends His deliverer as a baby to grow and learn the Egyptian ways. Moses got the very best education having been the grandson of Pharaoh. Pharaoh's daughter called his name Moses because she drew him out of the river. Moses grew and prospered in Egypt, but he had a longing for his people, the Hebrews. As with everything; providence would reign even in bad situations. One day Moses would find an Egyptian abusing one of his brethren and he killed him. This was not the way to handle the situation as the man had exposed his crime. Now Moses became a fugitive from Egypt and fled into the wilderness. This was the time when Moses would see the other side of the tracks as he would find a man and his daughters living in a place called Midian. There he would learn the humble occupation of Shepherd and would learn to shepherd people. Forty years would teach him to serve rather than to be served as he was in Egypt. In order to become a great leader, one must first learn to serve; otherwise there is a possibility that despotism would come to rule. This is the essence of God's kingdom because Jesus is the Good Shepherd and the Good Shepherd loves His sheep. Moses was in training to be a *great* leader, not just a leader. He would soon be asked to lead an enormous multitude of people out of Egypt and through the wilderness to the Promised Land. God had prepared Moses in leadership by having him to be raised in the royal family. God also taught him humility through his own mistakes that sent him to the wilderness, away from the privileged life with which he was accustomed. As you can see; providence had a major role in the development of greatness. You may think that you messed up at times, but providence is at work in the background to produce in you, something much greater than you might think. God is always at work in the lives of His children so that they can become all that He has ordained them to become. The seed of greatness in all of us is that desire to know the Lord our God. Moses needed all of the attributes that he acquired through his trials in order to lead this great multitude of people to freedom. God would use Moses to bring judgment upon Egypt for their great sin against His people and thus bring justice for them. After forty years, Moses encountered God in the form of a burning bush and was instructed to confront Pharaoh concerning the Hebrew people. Consider this; Moses comes before the most powerful leader in the known world to command him to let God's people go. Moses must have had nerves of steel to speak to someone that had the authority to have him destroyed even before he spoke the first word to him. He knew that God was with him and that no matter what happened that God would preserve him so that His word would prosper. Has God instructed you to do something? He will see you through it no matter what it may look like at the moment, because He told you to do it. Even in the midst of a shipwreck, God will forge for Himself a vessel to honor Him.

Act 27:21-25 KJV But after long abstinence Paul stood forth in the midst of them, and said, Sirs, ye should have hearkened unto me, and not have loosed from Crete, and to have gained this harm and loss. (22) And now I exhort you to be of good cheer: for there shall be no loss of any man's life among you, but of the ship. (23) For there stood by me this night the angel of God, whose I am, and whom I serve, (24) Saying, Fear not, Paul; thou must be brought before Caesar: and, lo, God hath given thee all them that sail with thee. (25) Wherefore, sirs, be of good cheer: for I believe God, that it shall be even as it was told me.

Paul didn't fear to die in the shipwreck because God had ordained him to go before Caesar and he knew that God would see that he made it. In the same manner, Moses was told to deliver the people out of the bondage of Egypt so he had to believe that God would make that happen, no matter what it looked like. This forms great character in a person, that he has faith in God against all odds. Your faith will push you far beyond the boundaries of earthly logic to a place of prominence in God's kingdom if you use it. Never think of your problems as more than you can handle. Faith in God and His command will prove to be greater than any obstacle that you may encounter. Moses faces off against Pharaoh and God works great miracles to bring about His purpose. In the end of this confrontation, Pharaoh expels the Hebrews from Egypt, but they don't go empty-handed. The

Hebrew people finally leave Egypt with much wealth and substance and begin their journey toward the Promised Land. There was an enormous multitude of people that left the land of Egypt that day and this would leave the economy of Egypt devastated. Now Pharaoh changes his mind and musters his armies to go and re-capture the Hebrew slaves to bring them back. God directs Moses to lead the people to a place by the Red Sea where they would be trapped between Pharaoh and the sea. As Moses and the people made their way through the wilderness, they came to a mountain range and through a place between two mountains. Just when all seemed good and they were moving further away from the land of their troubles, they cleared the backside of the mountain and came to an abrupt halt. They had come up against the Red Sea and the only visible way out was to return the way that they came. I can only imagine all of the complaining as the multitudes began to look at their circumstances. That is our problem when sometimes we begin to focus on all that is wrong and forget that God is an Awesome God. But then as if to face the sea wasn't enough; word came that the armies of Pharaoh were just behind them in hard pursuit. So now they're corralled between the mountains and the Red Sea and the only way out is now blocked by the armies of Pharaoh. Now the impossible had snared them like birds caught in a net. But this is where God makes Himself known; He works in the realm of impossibility. When mankind is faced with the impossible, he's helpless to do anything but seek God. This is God's will that we put our trust and faith in Him and believe in His grace and power to see us through. No matter what the circumstances; though they seem impossible; we must understand that there is nothing impossible with God. As Pharaoh's chariots moved in closer, there came out of heaven a pillar of fire that held back the evil pursuit of the enemy. This is a picture of the zeal of the children of God in our world today; we are to be fiery ministers of truth holding back the intentions of evil and it's pursuit of the souls of people. The fire held them through the night as God caused an east wind to blow upon the Red Sea. I can see the massive body of water blasted back and forth by this torrential wind as the gargantuan waves crash against the rocks disintegrating into the air. The roaring of the waves must have sounded like thunder as the mighty hand of God began to cause the waters to separate. Truly this was a colossal show of the immense power of almighty God. As the waters separated they formed massive walls on either side of a path of dry ground that there was a way through for the people. Where there was no way; God made a way. We should never give up hope because if God could part the mighty waters of the Red Sea, then our problems are no problem for Him. The people were facing certain death and once again God delivers them from its cold clammy grasp. God's desire is to deliver us from the grip of death whose fingers reach deep into the souls of people. God made a way for the people but He was not finished yet. When the last set of footprints made their way to the other side where their freedom awaited them, then God released the pillar of fire so that Pharaoh could continue his pursuit. But just as all of the armies of Pharaoh made their way into the midst of the sea; God released the waters and they came crashing down upon them. In one fatal swoop, God crushed the pursuing armies of Egypt and ended the bondage of Israel. Mankind could never credit himself or any natural occurrence for this deliverance because only God can make the impossible a possibility. What if you were faced with the kind of impossible tasks as Moses was, would you have the kind of faith to believe God for the answer? The time has come for all of us to show great faith in God and His purposes as did Moses. Moses is yet another light of strength on that pathway that helps us to understand the unfailing grace of God, that we might find greatness where we didn't see it before.

Joshua and Caleb

Moses sent twelve men to spy out the land of Canaan; two of them were Joshua and Caleb, the only ones that brought a good report. Ten of the men were fearful and had doubt about any conquest of the land. Now we can see something that displeases God. Ten men were fearful of the land that God had promised that He would give them. They knew that the Lord had promised to drive out the inhabitants of the land from before them. These men saw the giants and were afraid; they had no faith in God to conquer them and the people believed the bad report. God made them wander in the wilderness forty years until a whole generation died off.

Heb 3:15-19 KJV While it is said, To day if ye will hear his voice, harden not your hearts, as in the provocation. (16) For some, when they had heard, did provoke: howbeit not all that came out of Egypt by Moses. (17) But with whom was he grieved forty years? was it not with them that had sinned, whose carcases fell in the wilderness? (18) And to whom sware he that they should not enter into his rest, but to them that believed not? (19) So we see that they could not enter in because of unbelief.

Joshua and Caleb were the only two from their generation that would enter into the promised land. Joshua was the one to carry on the torch from Moses and it was he that led the nation into the promised land. The name Joshua means "the Lord our salvation" and the book that was named for him is a book of conquest. Joshua knew that they could defeat the giants of the land because he believed God's word. There came a day when God would visit Joshua and give him His word for strength:

Jos 1:1-6 KJV Now after the death of Moses the servant of the LORD it came to pass, that the LORD spake unto Joshua the son of Nun, Moses' minister, saying, (2) Moses my servant is dead; now therefore arise, go over this Jordan, thou, and all this people, unto the land which I do give to them, even to the children of Israel. (3) Every place that the sole of your foot shall tread upon, that have I given unto you, as I said unto Moses. (4) From the wilderness and this Lebanon even unto the great river, the river Euphrates, all the land of the Hittites, and unto the great sea toward the going down of the sun, shall be your coast. (5) There shall not any man be able to stand before thee all the days of thy life: as I was with Moses, so I will be with thee: I will not fail thee, nor forsake thee. (6) Be strong and of a good courage: for unto this people shalt thou divide for an inheritance the land, which I sware unto their fathers to give them.

Joshua was faithful in the days of Moses and now he is given the great honor to lead God's people into the Promised Land. Again if you're faithful in what He asks you to do, He will trust you with more. God seeks for people that will be faithful to Him and He is the creator of the universe. There is nothing impossible with God and if you face giants, then trust in God to give you the power to overcome them. Joshua was now facing an enormous task in leading great multitudes into a conquest for the land. The thing that the ten other spies were so afraid of doing was now in the hands of Joshua and he forges ahead without fear. There may have been giants in the land, but there came a fear of the Israelites all across the land so that nations fainted because of the terror of them.

Jos 2:9 KJV And she said unto the men, I know that the LORD hath given you the land, and that your terror is fallen upon us, and that all the inhabitants of the land faint because of you.

One person can make a difference between victory or failure. Joshua was a leader that had followed

Moses command in the past and now that command was his. He learned to fear the Lord and to trust in Him with what today would be called blind faith. Do you want to move the heart of God?; then have faith in Him. Now there came a time when Joshua would have to trust in God with this blind faith in the conquest of Jericho. This was a fortified city that was impenetrable with great walls that protected it. This to a non-believer would be absolutely impossible to accomplish and he would turn away. God would conquer this city as He would instruct Joshua to do something that could only be considered the hand of God.

Jos 6:1-5 KJV Now Jericho was straitly shut up because of the children of Israel: none went out, and none came in. (2) And the LORD said unto Joshua, See, I have given into thine hand Jericho, and the king thereof, and the mighty men of valour. (3) And ye shall compass the city, all ye men of war, and go round about the city once. Thus shalt thou do six days. (4) And seven priests shall bear before the ark seven trumpets of rams' horns: and the seventh day ye shall compass the city seven times, and the priests shall blow with the trumpets. (5) And it shall come to pass, that when they make a long blast with the ram's horn, and when ye hear the sound of the trumpet, all the people shall shout with a great shout; and the wall of the city shall fall down flat, and the people shall ascend up every man straight before him.

This is not the way that men would approach this

situation and to them, it might seem to be insane. Joshua was the leader of a nation of people and his choice was to believe God. Men would choose battering rams and ladders and fiery arrows and anything else that might cause damage to the occupants inside, but this would not be necessary for Joshua. This was God's conquest and it is He that will have the glory of it. Joshua obeyed God and sent his men to compass the city for six days and as commanded they did this seven times on the seventh day and blew the trumpets and shouted. The wall fell as God had said and the armies went up for the victory. Now we can see why that the nations were afraid of them because God was with them and miracles were their victories. This would not have been the case if there were no leaders to obey God. The most important man in the nation was in complete submission to the Lord. Can you imagine the ridicule that he encountered as he instructed the men to do this thing seven days? This must have seemed too crazy to many people and they would have condemned the leader for it. You must be willing to believe God above all that the world would disagree with you about; this is the seed of greatness. You can spend your life in comfort and complacency because God has given you a free will. He is a gentleman and won't impede on your decisions, but if you have faith in Him, then He can work miracles through you. You may try and fail time and time again, but one day your faith will result in the impossible and you will be the instrument of God's glory.

There was another man that brought a good report against the other ten spies and that was Caleb. He was willing to fight the giants with Joshua and he was the other of the two of his generation that would enter the Promised Land. His good report showed that he had faith in God and God would preserve him so that he could receive his inheritance in the Promised Land. In the original report, they said that they looked like grasshoppers in the sight of these giants. Consider that this to the unbeliever would be a task not ever taken because of the enormity of the enemy. Again an impossible situation that the average person will and did turn away from. Joshua and Caleb were men of faith and were not shaken by this intimidating situation. Caleb waited forty years for the opportunity to act on his faith because of those that didn't believe. Now the time had come for him to make his move. As Joshua was assigning territories to the tribes; Caleb came to him to ask for his.

Jos 14:6-13 KJV Then the children of Judah came unto Joshua in Gilgal: and Caleb the son of Jephunneh the Kenezite said unto him, Thou knowest the thing that the LORD said unto Moses the man of God concerning me and thee in Kadeshbarnea. (7) Forty years old was I when Moses the servant of the LORD sent me from Kadeshbarnea to espy out the land; and I brought him word again as it was in mine heart. (8) Nevertheless my brethren that went up with me made the heart of the people melt: but I wholly followed the LORD my God. (9) And Moses sware on that day, saying, Surely the land whereon thy feet have trodden shall be thine inheritance, and thy children's for ever, because thou hast wholly followed the LORD my God. (10) And now, behold, the LORD hath kept me alive, as he said, these forty and five years, even since the LORD spake this word unto Moses, while the children of Israel wandered in the wilderness: and now, lo, I am this day fourscore and five years old. (11) As yet I am as strong this day as I was in the day that Moses sent me: as my strength was then, even so is my strength now, for war, both to go out, and to come in. (12) Now therefore give me this mountain, whereof the LORD spake in that day; for thou heardest in that day how the Anakims were there, and that the cities were great and fenced: if so be the LORD will be with me, then I shall be able to drive them out, as the LORD said. (13) And Joshua blessed him, and gave unto Caleb the son of Jephunneh Hebron for an inheritance.

This is very impressive that this eighty-five year old man desires to lead his people to conquer the giants and take the land. Caleb believed God and God preserved his strength and rewarded his faithfulness. He is an icon of faith in my heart because he never grew weary of his goal, even in

49

his old age. Nothing is impossible with God and age is no factor in God's purposes. You don't have to be young to be virile and strong if you have faith in God. The world has a pattern of aging that they adhere to very strictly and we see the results of faith in those patterns. Caleb did not follow that pattern, but rather he set his heart to God's pattern which disagrees with the world. When will we find that great faith like these true believers that got their victories against impossible odds? Two more lights now in that pathway that illuminate the steps to greatness can become the inspiration for the rest of us to forge a life that glorifies God.

Rahab

There was another faithful witness in the time of Joshua that deserves mention and her name is Rahab. There came a time when Joshua had sent two spies to spy out the territory of Jericho. They were to be inconspicuous and blend in so as not to be recognized. A friend in a home bible study said that to visit a harlot's house wouldn't be noticed much as men came and went on a regular basis. That would explain why they went to the harlot in the first place. Rahab; when she found out who these men were, began to tell them of the great fear in the land of the terror of the Israelites, in so doing she gave them confidence.

Jos 2:9-11 KJV And she said unto the men, I know that the LORD hath given you the land, and that your terror is fallen upon us, and that all the inhabitants of the land faint because of you. (10) For we have heard how the LORD dried up the water of the Red sea for you, when ye came out of Egypt; and what ye did unto the two kings of the Amorites, that were on the other side Jordan, Sihon and Og, whom ye utterly destroyed. (11) And as soon as we had heard these things, our hearts did melt, neither did there remain any more courage in any man, because of you: for the LORD your God, he is God in heaven above, and in earth beneath.

Somehow, word came to the king of Jericho that there were two Israelite spies that had come to spy out the country. He sent a message to Rahab to have her expose the men but she said that they waited until the evening about the time when the gates were to be shut and they left and she didn't know where they went. She told them to go after them quickly that they would catch them. Here was a citizen of Jericho and it would have been very easy for her to have these men arrested. She sent the pursuers on a wild goose chase to protect the spies and buy them some time. Rahab showed faith in the God of the Hebrews in that she sided with the spies. She had the wisdom to make a deal with these men for the safety of her and her family. Rahab believed that God would help them to take the city and she acted according to her faith. In face of danger of losing her life, she hid the strangers on the roof so that they could escape the hand of death. They made the deal with her that if she would hang a scarlet cord in her window that everyone inside the house would be spared. By faith, Rahab had saved her family from imminent destruction by her actions. This isn't the end of the story, however. At some time in the future, she married a man named Salmon from the tribe of Judah and had a son by the name of Boaz the kinsman redeemer that married Ruth the Great-grandmother of David. In this, the faith of Rahab made her become named in the lineage of Jesus the Messiah. This is a great honor that one would be included in the word of God as one that helped God's people. Not only that but Rahab was a great witness to that fact that God can and will use the least likely for His purposes. Now we have another light in the pathway that illuminates the faith that it takes to do great works in the earth. Can we become outstanding in the timeline of God's plan? If we can learn from history and trust in the miraculous power of God, then like Rahab we also can be remembered for great faith.

David

One day, long ago there was a young boy out in the fields tending his father's sheep. As young boys do, he was probably filling his time with as much fun as he could muster in the fields. His eye was pretty good with a sling and he more than likely spent days practicing with it to become an expert, having so much time on his hands. He was a responsible boy as he kept his father's sheep from danger even at the risk of his own welfare. He protected the sheep from wild beasts with only his staff and a sling. This young boy was developing courage and integrity as he had respect for his father to do so well the task with which he was entrusted. He was the youngest and least of his brothers of which there were seven. One day God had determined to select the king's replacement because King Saul had disobeyed the command of the Lord and did an abominable thing in the sight of the people. God could no longer trust the king and had already selected for himself another. Saul was the first king of Israel, but he was the choice of the people as he stood head and shoulder above everyone else. It may have been that to the people he was the logical choice because of his great stature and looked like a strong man. He was humble at the beginning and did many exploits in defeating Israel's enemies, but time and notoriety would draw out the true nature of his heart. God had already seen a noble and faithful heart that was truly a vessel of courage, integrity and righteous judgment. God sent faithful Samuel to anoint His new king. As it would happen the seven brothers of this boy were the logical choices to be examined for king as they were strong and of good stature.

1Sa 16:6-11 KJV And it came to pass, when they were come, that he looked on Eliab, and said, Surely the LORD'S anointed is before him. (7) But the LORD said unto Samuel, Look not on his countenance, or on the height of his stature; because I have refused him: for the LORD seeth not as man seeth; for man looketh on the outward appearance, but the LORD looketh on the heart. (8) Then Jesse called Abinadab, and made him pass before Samuel. And he said, Neither hath the LORD chosen this. (9) Then Jesse made Shammah to pass by. And he said, Neither hath the LORD chosen this. (10) Again, Jesse made seven of his sons to pass before Samuel. And Samuel said unto Jesse, The LORD hath not chosen these. (11) And Samuel said unto Jesse, Are here all thy children? And he said, There remaineth yet the youngest, and, behold, he keepeth the sheep. And Samuel said unto Jesse, Send and fetch him: for we will not sit down till he come hither.

This was the same way that the people chose Saul; he was tall and fair to look at and seemed to be the right one. As these brothers were impressive to look at and each was a logical choice. God, however, did not choose the king in this manner. I once knew a man that was very small in stature and I worked with him many times. Each time I got to know him better, he seemed larger and more impressive. After much time I realized that this man was bigger than all of the tallest men that I knew and it was not his stature, but his heart. He had a heart of gold or you could say that he had the heart of a king and I'll never forget him. This was the kind of man that God had chosen because of his heart. They sent for this boy and Samuel would hear from God of His choice.

1Sa 16:12-13 KJV And he sent, and brought him in. Now he was ruddy, and withal of a beautiful countenance, and goodly to look to. And the LORD said, Arise, anoint him: for this is he. (13) Then Samuel took the horn of oil, and anointed him in the midst of his brethren: and the Spirit of the LORD came upon David from that day forward. So Samuel rose up, and went to Ramah.

God didn't look at David's stature but saw a willing vessel that was passionate for righteousness and justice, and most of all he trusted God. David had humble beginnings but reflected his determination to see God's righteousness prevail. Where do you stand today? In this world of injustice and calling evil good and good evil do you have a heart for righteousness? David had the kind of heart that God could use to change a nation and He did.

There was a time when Saul and his army were in a standoff against their enemy the Philistines. The Philistines had a champion that was very great in stature and well trained at killing. He was a giant warrior that put fear in the hearts of Saul and all of his men. This champion was loud and boastful and was disrespectful of the God of the Hebrews and he made a challenge to Israel.

1Sa 17:8-11 KJV And he stood and cried unto the armies of Israel, and said unto them, Why are ye come out to set your battle in array? am not I a Philistine, and ye servants to Saul? choose you a man for you, and let him come down to me. (9) If he be able to fight with me, and to kill me, then will we be your servants: but if I prevail against him, and kill him, then shall ye be our servants, and serve us. (10) And the Philistine said, I defy the armies of Israel this day; give me a man, that we may fight together. (11) When Saul and all Israel heard those words of the Philistine, they were dismayed, and greatly afraid.

Intimidation seems to work well because fear is a very debilitating spirit. Fear can win battles in the right circumstances because it can physically drain the body of strength. These Philistines were using it to their advantage so as to avert a battle and still get the victory. Providence, however, would win the day because they didn't expect what would come very soon to meet their challenge. David's three eldest brothers were there at the camp with Saul and Jesse sent food to them by the hand of David. Now David, when he entered the camp heard this boastful Philistine named Goliath of Gath and was angry at him because he insulted the army of the God of his fathers. You see, David had a different perspective than anyone else because he was concerned with the integrity of God's people and not himself. For David, fear was not an option as he had faith in God more than anyone else. David would stand for justice that day and his motive was to restore the integrity of Israel. When all of Israel's army and his own brothers would not fight with this giant; David would go to Saul to volunteer to fight on behalf of Israel. This, the youngest and the least of his brothers would rise to this occasion in meeting this arrogant monstrosity. The words of David reveal a heart of courage and persistence.

1Sa 17:41-46 KJV And the Philistine came on and drew near unto David; and the man that bare the shield went before him. (42) And when the

Philistine looked about, and saw David, he disdained him: for he was but a youth, and ruddy, and of a fair countenance. (43) And the Philistine said unto David, Am I a dog, that thou comest to me with staves? And the Philistine cursed David by his gods. (44) And the Philistine said to David, Come to me, and I will give thy flesh unto the fowls of the air, and to the beasts of the field. (45) Then said David to the Philistine, Thou comest to me with a sword, and with a spear, and with a shield: but I come to thee in the name of the LORD of hosts, the God of the armies of Israel, whom thou hast defied. (46) This day will the LORD deliver thee into mine hand; and I will smite thee, and take thine head from thee; and I will give the carcases of the host of the Philistines this day unto the fowls of the air, and to the wild beasts of the earth; that all the earth may know that there is a God in Israel.

These selfless words that defend the righteous God of Israel are backed by a determined heart that wields the personification of greatness. David had a righteous cause and was willing to die for his God and his countrymen. This Philistine giant had nothing of that sort in that his arrogant purpose was for his own glory. This fight was truly uneven looking at this tiny boy standing with a sling in the dust cloud before an enormous murdering giant with his array of death implements. It was uneven because David had the real advantage against his evil adversary. David walked by the mighty hand of

God which is much greater than even a thousand Goliath's. On this day, providence would reveal the heart of a true king before the armies of Israel. David would use the skill that he honed in the fields while tending his father's sheep and would fire a stone between the eyes of this warrior that was so intimidating. When the giant fell, David ran to him, took out Goliath's own sword and removed his head. This young boy that came out against impossible odds, came without fear and used the courage that came with faith in God and defeated the enemy that even the mightiest warriors were afraid to battle. With God, all things are possible because if we trust in Him there is nothing that can hinder our courage. There is much arrogance today in the world that defies the God of the universe and we are His vessels. Will we have that same determined heart as did David on that day? Will we be like that army that feared the giant? We must learn to see the true value of selfless sacrifice for the glory of God and do justice without fear.

David grew and his popularity grew with the people and Saul would one day become David's father-in-law. There came a day, however, that Saul began to see David as a threat to his throne. Saul knew in his heart that David was God's choice and that he would one day replace him. Saul was in defiance of God and was determined that the throne would go to his own son. Saul became obsessed with killing David and began a pursuit that would last for years. David had six hundred men under his leadership and they lived a life running from Saul and his armies. This doesn't look like a king's life, always on the run and hiding from Saul, but David had respect for his father-in-law the king. You see David had respect for Saul's office and would not kill Saul because he was anointed of God. David would not touch God's anointed because that is best left to God. David had two opportunities to kill Saul and did not do it, but brought these to Saul's attention to show him that he was not his enemy. There came a time when David and his men went to the Philistines and David acquired Ziklag for a dwelling place for himself and his men and their families, where Saul wouldn't pursue. But one day David and his men were called to fight with the Philistines against the armies of Israel. This would be an awkward situation but David had to show intent to serve the king of the Philistines, so they went to the place of gathering to be counted. Providence would again intercede for David in that the military leaders of the Philistines refused to include David and his men for fear of them changing sides in battle. David and his men were sent back home and didn't have to fight against their own people. Can you see God's hand at work here? However, when they returned to Ziklag, they found their homes burned and all of their families kidnapped and their substance was stolen. Now there were six hundred of the toughest warriors around and they wept until they had no more strength to weep. These mighty men then directed their grief into anger against David and desired to kill him. David's heart was the inspiration for his great exploits and this time would be no different.

1Sa 30:6 KJV And David was greatly distressed; for the people spake of stoning him, because the soul of all the people was grieved, every man for his sons and for his daughters: but David encouraged himself in the LORD his God.

David turned to the source of valiance and integrity and hope; he turned to the Lord God for encouragement. He enquired of the Lord and He told David that he would recover all and to pursue the enemy. Two hundred of David's men were worn out and could not go on so David and four hundred men pursued after the Amalekites that had done this great evil against them. As it happened the Amalekites were defeated at the hand of David and his men and they recovered all as the Lord had said. They recovered all that they had lost but they also recovered everything that the Amalekites had taken before they invaded Ziklag and so there was great wealth acquired that day and they headed back to Ziklag. When they returned they were met by the two hundred men that stayed behind.

1Sa 30:21-22 KJV And David came to the two hundred men, which were so faint that they could not follow David, whom they had made also to abide at the brook Besor: and they went forth to meet David, and to meet the people that were with him: and when David came near to the people, he saluted them. (22) Then answered all the wicked men and men of Belial, of those that went with David, and said, Because they went not with us, we will not give them ought of the spoil that we have recovered, save to every man his wife and his children, that they may lead them away, and depart.

David would not allow that and said that everyone would receive the same because it was God that got them the victory and he made it a rule from then on. This is the difference between the heart of a man and the heart of a king.

1Sa 30:23-25 KJV Then said David, Ye shall not do so, my brethren, with that which the LORD hath given us, who hath preserved us, and delivered the company that came against us into our hand. (24) For who will hearken unto you in this matter? but as his part is that goeth down to the battle, so shall his part be that tarrieth by the stuff: they shall part alike. (25) And it was so from that day forward, that he made it a statute and an ordinance for Israel unto this day.

During all this time as the Philistines fought against Israel; Saul and his sons were killed in battle and so now again providence would prevail for the one that would be king. David and his men went throughout Judah giving gifts of the wealth that they had acquired and returned to Ziklag. Two days later news of Saul and his sons came to David and he lamented for them. David would soon become king over Judah seven years and after that, he would be made king over all of Israel. David became the greatest king that Israel would know until Messiah would come. Throughout the books of the Old Testament, God compares all of the kings against David and he became the reference point for the scriptures as to righteousness and justice. Here is yet another light that shines on the pathway brightly to guide you and me to a place of God's favor and greatness.

Hezekiah

During a time after which Israel and Judah had become two kingdoms, a very trying time had come for Hezekiah the king of Judah. The Assyrian king had been conquering the nations and destroying their cities with determined force. He had already taken the northern kingdom Israel and exiled the inhabitants to Assyria and continued his conquest of territories and now had his sights on Judah and Jerusalem. The knowledge of the conquest of the Assyrians and their victories was a weapon in itself used of the generals of the king of Assyria to put fear into their victims. This was a dark time for the northern kingdom that had sinned against God and was carried away and now had become a test for King Hezekiah of the southern kingdom of

Judah. Hezekiah's father Ahaz did wickedly against God and had set up high places where they worshipped idols and false gods. They were also worshiping the brazen serpent that Moses had made during the exodus from Egypt. When Hezekiah ascended to the throne he was a believer in the true and living God of Abraham, Isaac, and Jacob. He did things that pleased the Lord and was a good king in God's eyes.

2Ki 18:1-3 KJV Now it came to pass in the third year of Hoshea son of Elah king of Israel, that Hezekiah the son of Ahaz king of Judah began to reign. (2) Twenty and five years old was he when he began to reign; and he reigned twenty and nine years in Jerusalem. His mother's name also was Abi, the daughter of Zachariah. (3) And he did that which was right in the sight of the LORD, according to all that David his father did.

When a person puts his faith in God against the common flow, he pleases God. Complacency in any form of leadership is like cancer that destroys from within. When you stand against evil, God stands with you because evil destroys people. We all know right from wrong because God has given each of us a measure of faith and a conscience. To do wrong is a conscious rebellion against God's will and to follow after wrong ways is destructive to others around us. Hezekiah inherited a kingdom of idolatry and rebellion against God. What is the heart of a king? As we have already seen through David; the heart of a true king is to seek first the

God of the universe and to adhere to righteousness and justice. David honored the office of king and knew the great privilege and challenge to serve as king. Hezekiah also understood the honor and privilege of serving God in the capacity of a shepherd of His people. He knew what he had to do as he entered into service as king of Judah concerning the will of God. He began by destroying the sources of evil in the kingdom.

2Ki 18:4-6 KJV He removed the high places, and brake the images, and cut down the groves, and brake in pieces the brasen serpent that Moses had made: for unto those days the children of Israel did burn incense to it: and he called it Nehushtan. (5) He trusted in the LORD God of Israel; so that after him was none like him among all the kings of Judah, nor any that were before him. (6) For he clave to the LORD, and departed not from following him, but kept his commandments, which the LORD commanded Moses.

This is the kind of leadership that pleases God as you can see that the word of God illuminates Hezekiah in a good light. We all have an opportunity to please God by removing every destructive behavior from our lives and to learn God's ways and to walk in them. We have the power to do so today by trusting in Jesus Christ and walking in righteousness. Sin has been defeated for the Christian so we have an advantage that Hezekiah didn't possess at the time. You can see the efforts of King Hezekiah as he fought sin and evil ways in his day. How much more in our day can we do, seeing that God dwells in us. The ways of man are evil and to follow after righteousness is a hindrance to those ways, so you become an enemy to the way of the world.

Hezekiah did that which was right in the eyes of God and as usual, Satan sends his messenger to attempt to destroy what Hezekiah had done. There came a time after the death of the Assyrian king Sargon, when his son Sennacherib came to power, that many of the territories began a campaign of independence from Assyrian oppression. Hezekiah would join in the rebellion because he worked towards independence for his kingdom and the tribute that he had to pay to Assyria was very large. The messengers come to first offer a deal and to instill fear into the king and his people.

2Ki 18:17-20 KJV And the king of Assyria sent Tartan and Rabsaris and Rabshakeh from Lachish to king Hezekiah with a great host against Jerusalem. And they went up and came to Jerusalem. And when they were come up, they came and stood by the conduit of the upper pool, which is in the highway of the fuller's field. (18) And when they had called to the king, there came out to them Eliakim the son of Hilkiah, which was over the household, and Shebna the scribe, and Joah the son of Asaph the recorder. (19) And Rabshakeh said unto them, Speak ye now to Hezekiah, Thus saith the great king, the king of Assyria, What confidence is this wherein thou trustest? (20) Thou sayest, (but they are but vain words,) I have counsel and strength for the war. Now on whom dost thou trust, that thou rebellest against me?

Rabshakeh had no fear of Hezekiah's God and his heart was evil and in defiance of Him. Today is no different in that the politically correct are in defiance of the ways of God and have no respect for Him or His people. Political correctness boasts of tolerance but does in no way tolerate Christianity. As long as evil is in the world, there will always be resistance to righteousness. Hezekiah had very much pressure to give up and give in to the powers of wickedness.

2Ki 18:23-25 KJV Now therefore, I pray thee, give pledges to my lord the king of Assyria, and I will deliver thee two thousand horses, if thou be able on thy part to set riders upon them. (24) How then wilt thou turn away the face of one captain of the least of my master's servants, and put thy trust on Egypt for chariots and for horsemen? (25) Am I now come up without the LORD against this place to destroy it? The LORD said to me, Go up against this land, and destroy it.

Rabshakeh lies in that he tells them that God told him to destroy them. Now he is on Hezekiah's territory and through him, Satan tries to cause fear to take him down. Evil will lie to anyone to accomplish the goal for which it is set to fulfill. However, Hezekiah is not moved at lies because he is in God's favor and he will seek the wisdom of God through Isaiah the Prophet.

Now Rabshakeh was speaking in the language of the Hebrews and the people on the wall heard and understood his warnings. This was purposeful so that fear could find its way to the general public. Satan uses fear to hinder the advancement of God's program for His people and to destroy faith. You see faith is an effective weapon against the unrighteous works of evil and without faith in God one is defeated already.

2Ki 18:28-32 KJV Then Rabshakeh stood and cried with a loud voice in the Jews' language, and spake, saying, Hear the word of the great king, the king of Assyria: (29) Thus saith the king, Let not Hezekiah deceive you: for he shall not be able to deliver you out of his hand: (30) Neither let Hezekiah make you trust in the LORD, saying, The LORD will surely deliver us, and this city shall not be delivered into the hand of the king of Assyria. (31) Hearken not to Hezekiah: for thus saith the king of Assyria, Make an agreement with me by a present, and come out to me, and then eat ye every man of his own vine, and every one of his fig tree, and drink ye every one the waters of his cistern: (32) Until I come and take you away to a land like your own land, a land of corn and wine, a land of bread and vineyards, a land of oil olive and of honey, that ye may live, and not die: and hearken not unto Hezekiah, when he persuadeth you, saying, The LORD will deliver us.

This attitude is quite common in our day in that the faithful are ridiculed for their faith and looked upon as someone that believes in fairytales. They can't understand the ways of a godly person. However, when they speak evil of us then we can be grateful because we have a great reward in Heaven.

Luk 6:22-23 KJV Blessed are ye, when men shall hate you, and when they shall separate you from their company, and shall reproach you, and cast out your name as evil, for the Son of man's sake. (23) Rejoice ye in that day, and leap for joy: for, behold, your reward is great in heaven: for in the like manner did their fathers unto the prophets.

This puts the devout Christian in good company with King Hezekiah as he had the reputation of serving God at the irritation of his enemies. We must pray for those that ridicule us because we know their end if they don't find the love of Christ.

Hezekiah gets word of the evil intent of the Assyrian king that no gods can deliver any of the nations.

2Ki 18:33-37 KJV Hath any of the gods of the nations delivered at all his land out of the hand of the king of Assyria? (34) Where are the gods of Hamath, and of Arpad? where are the gods of Sepharvaim, Hena, and Ivah? have they delivered Samaria out of mine hand? (35) Who are they among all the gods of the countries, that have delivered their country out of mine hand, that the LORD should deliver Jerusalem out of mine hand? (36) But the people held their peace, and answered him not a word: for the king's commandment was, saying, Answer him not. (37) Then came Eliakim the son of Hilkiah, which was over the household, and Shebna the scribe, and Joah the son of Asaph the recorder, to Hezekiah with their clothes rent, and told him the words of Rabshakeh.

Now the people are afraid, but they obey the command of the king and now it's time for Hezekiah to act. The first thing that he will do is to seek God's wisdom and that is what makes him a great king.

2Ki 19:1-2 KJV And it came to pass, when king Hezekiah heard it, that he rent his clothes, and covered himself with sackcloth, and went into the house of the LORD. (2) And he sent Eliakim, which was over the household, and Shebna the scribe, and the elders of the priests, covered with sackcloth, to Isaiah the prophet the son of Amoz.

This is a good lesson for all of us; when we have a situation, we should first seek God's wisdom on the matter. Hezekiah trusted in the Lord and as his faith was, he will obey the word of God, no matter what the situation looks like. Isaiah gives comfort to the king by the word of God so that he will have the courage to resist the evil threats and stand in the face of adversity.

Eph 6:13 KJV Wherefore take unto you the whole armour of God, that ye may be able to withstand in the evil day, and having done all, to stand.

No matter what happens, there is hope in Christ and when the hour is darkest, that is when we must stand fast in the faith. Hezekiah is the king and all the people are watching him; what he does now will affect the way that people encounter God or if they will turn from Him.

The messengers return with a threatening letter to Hezekiah reminding him of their victories over the gods of the other nations. The letter spoke of the strong nations that had fallen at their hands and that his God wouldn't deliver him from their wrath. What is the thing that Hezekiah does with this letter? He spread it out before the Lord and prayed to Him with his whole heart. Prayer is the communication with the God of the universe and is our weapon of mass destruction to the evil report. God listens to the prayers of His people and He will move Heaven and earth to accomplish good according to His will.

2Ki 19:20 KJV Then Isaiah the son of Amoz sent to Hezekiah, saying, Thus saith the LORD God of Israel, That which thou hast prayed to me against Sennacherib king of Assyria I have heard.

God had a word for Sennacherib in that He reminds him that Israel has despised him and laughed at him. He then gives him the reason and that is his pride against the true and living God. God rebukes the king of Assyria because of pride and arrogance and vain words. God is only moved to anger by the hurtful words of prideful men.

Jas 4:6 KJV But he giveth more grace. Wherefore he saith, God resisteth the proud, but giveth grace unto the humble.

God would fight for Hezekiah in a very supernatural way because He is moved by faith and the next morning would reveal just how much He was moved.

2Ki 19:32-37 KJV Therefore thus saith the LORD concerning the king of Assyria, He shall not come into this city, nor shoot an arrow there, nor come before it with shield, nor cast a bank against it. (33) By the way that he came, by the same shall he return, and shall not come into this city, saith the LORD. (34) For I will defend this city, to save it, for mine own sake, and for my servant David's sake. (35) And it came to pass that night, that the angel of the LORD went out, and smote in the camp of the Assyrians an hundred fourscore and five thousand: and when they arose early in the morning, behold, they were all dead corpses. (36) So Sennacherib king of Assyria departed, and went and returned, and dwelt at Nineveh. (37) And it came to pass, as he was worshipping in the house of Nisroch his god, that Adrammelech and Sharezer his sons smote him with the sword: and they escaped into the land of Armenia. And Esarhaddon his son reigned in his stead.

God's favor is unlimited and when He does something, He does it right. Hezekiah's faith was rewarded and he didn't have to lift a sword, but his enemy was wiped out. The heart of a true king is one of great faith in God and a life that reveals that faith in the face of adversity. Hezekiah is another light in that pathway that teaches us how that God can move in big ways when we have faith for the impossible.

Josiah

As it would happen, human nature and the propensity to sin had once again brought the kingdom of Judah to a low level and darkness reigned as idol worship came to replace faith in God. Hezekiah's son Manasseh became king at twelve years old and reigned for fifty-five years. But he did evil in the sight of God and brought about this idol worship and abominations of the heathen of the land. There came a time in which Manasseh would see the light as he was bound in chains and fetters and brought to Babylon. He humbled himself and prayed to God and God delivered him and brought him back to Jerusalem. He began to restore the kingdom; he built a great wall around the city and took the idol worship out of the temple and put them out of the city. However, he was still faced with problems in that the people were still worshiping false gods in the high places. He was too late in his repentance for his son and after his death; his son came to the throne and did evil in the sight of God.

2Ch 33:21-25 KJV Amon was two and twenty years old when he began to reign, and reigned two years in Jerusalem. (22) But he did that which was evil in the sight of the LORD, as did Manasseh his father: for Amon sacrificed unto all the carved images which Manasseh his father had made, and served them; (23) And humbled not himself before the LORD, as Manasseh his father had humbled himself; but Amon trespassed more and more. (24) And his servants conspired against him, and slew him in his own house. (25) But the people of the land slew all them that had conspired against king Amon; and the people of the land made Josiah his son king in his stead.

Evil is always a gamble and in Amon's case, it was a gamble that he lost. He reigned a very short time and someone saw the destructive behavior as a threat to the kingdom as it truly was. I don't know what must have been in the heart of Josiah as he saw his father destroying the way of life that his grandfather had instituted after his conversion, but it must have either changed or solidified his worldview. Josiah was eight years old when he ascended to the throne and at age sixteen in his eighth year as king, he began to seek after God. He did that which was right in the sight of God as it says; "like his father David". In Josiah's twelfth year being king, he set his face to rid the kingdom of idol worship. He destroyed all of the graven images and the high places and everything that represented evil in the sight of God. Have you cleaned your house? Is there any idolatry in your life? Jesus desires that we lose our life in order to save it. That means that we must turn away from our destructive lifestyle and clean out anything that is offensive to that which is right and good. Consider that everything that comes from evil that you entertain will dim your light and that will affect people around you. In Josiah's case; he took away everything that would cause people to sin against God. Sin desires to rule you and you must close the door to it and stand for righteousness. Josiah had a great responsibility and he made a decision and followed it through. He probably had many that were rejoicing at his actions, but there probably were those that became his enemies as well. Josiah had begun a building project to repair the temple of the Lord. He commanded that all of the money that was collected at the door of the temple was to be used to pay the builders and the artists in the repair of the breaches. Josiah was on a campaign to rebuild the relationship of his people to God. Now there came a day when the high priest had found the book of the law of God and had it to be presented to the king. How tragic that was; that the people had so forgotten God that they lost the books that were God's commandments to make them a great people. They no longer knew God but had gone astray because of the wickedness of the previous kings. This shows that a person's actions can make a difference in the lives of others insomuch as it can change the future. The previous kings had selfishly instigated their own sinful ways upon the kingdom and had a very destructive result on the collective minds and hearts of their subordinates. Some people may look up to you as a source of wisdom and trust your words. This comes with responsibility in that your personal gripes will become theirs. Your light will reflect in them but so also will any darkness. If you are in leadership, you must remain true to God's will, because you'll be held accountable to God for the people that you influenced; bad or good. Josiah was cleaning up the mess that his father and grandfather had created; this made him great. His eye was single and he didn't sway from the path and the light that was in him was not darkness.

Mat 6:22-23 KJV The light of the body is the eye: if therefore thine eye be single, thy whole body shall be full of light. (23) But if thine eye be evil, thy whole body shall be full of darkness. If therefore the light that is in thee be darkness, how great is that darkness!

Commitment is the word for this as Josiah was truly committed to bringing his kingdom into favor with God. Now when the books of the law were read to Josiah, he tore his clothes which means that he was grieved to find that they had drifted so far away from God's will. Josiah would go to the source of life and righteousness for His word concerning their fate.

2Ki 22:13 KJV Go ye, enquire of the LORD for me, and for the people, and for all Judah, concerning the words of this book that is found: for great is the wrath of the LORD that is kindled against us, because our fathers have not hearkened unto the words of this book, to do according unto all that which is written concerning us.

They inquired of the prophetess to give them the word of God concerning what will become of them. The word came that God would judge the nation because of their sinful ways and blatant idol worship, however, God is merciful and gives grace to the humble and He gave word to the king:

2Ki 22:18-20 KJV But to the king of Judah which sent you to enquire of the LORD, thus shall ye say to him, Thus saith the LORD God of Israel, As touching the words which thou hast heard; (19) Because thine heart was tender, and thou hast humbled thyself before the LORD, when thou heardest what I spake against this place, and against the inhabitants thereof, that they should become a desolation and a curse, and hast rent thy clothes, and wept before me; I also have heard thee, saith the LORD. (20) Behold therefore, I will gather thee unto thy fathers, and thou shalt be gathered into thy grave in peace;

and thine eyes shall not see all the evil which I will bring upon this place. And they brought the king word again.

God; for the sake of the humble king that repented for the nation would not bring the judgment in his day while he was alive. Judgment is averted by the heart of a king; one man that has faith in God and truly desires to walk according to God's will. How is your heart today; do you mourn for the lost and the wicked that are on a road to destruction? Do you mourn for a nation that has gone astray? Your prayers avail much whether you know it or not because God is listening to the humble cries of the righteous. Josiah was heard of God for his heart and not politics or any other reason. The heart is the center of the person and is who we truly are. It doesn't matter what you look like or what you are like in public; it matters what is in your heart.

2Ki 23:1-3 KJV And the king sent, and they gathered unto him all the elders of Judah and of Jerusalem. (2) And the king went up into the house of the LORD, and all the men of Judah and all the inhabitants of Jerusalem with him, and the priests, and the prophets, and all the people, both small and great: and he read in their ears all the words of the book of the covenant which was found in the house of the LORD. (3) And the king stood by a pillar, and made a covenant before the LORD, to walk after the LORD, and to keep his commandments and his testimonies and his statutes with all their heart and all their soul, to perform the words of this covenant that were written in this book. And all the people stood to the covenant.

Josiah's heart was aligned with true greatness in that he had been given a great honor to rule God's people and he made the changes that pleased God. When I was at my lowest in this life, I had to make a decision concerning the future. I turned to Jesus Christ and began to seek after Him and His kingdom. I concluded that the very best thing that I could do for my family, was to get myself right with God. This is the beginning for all of us in that we must start by seeking God and to become His sons and daughters and then God will do the rest as He leads us to greater heights.

Josiah after he made his decree then proceeded to reinstitute the Passover. This Passover would be the largest and most remembered of all.

2Ch 35:18-19 KJV And there was no passover like to that kept in Israel from the days of Samuel the prophet; neither did all the kings of Israel keep such a passover as Josiah kept, and the priests, and the Levites, and all Judah and Israel that were present, and the inhabitants of Jerusalem. (19) In the eighteenth year of the reign of Josiah was this passover kept.

Josiah, as you can see, had a true heart for God and compassion for people to bring them back to God. This is truly a man that was the least in that he used his great authority not to benefit himself, but to save a nation from the brink of disaster. He served God and that is the true source of greatness in this world.

2Ki 23:25 KJV And like unto him was there no king before him, that turned to the LORD with all his heart, and with all his soul, and with all his might, according to all the law of Moses; neither after him arose there any like him.

Here is yet another bright light to line the pathway to greatness in this life and beyond. Josiah shows how the heart of one person can change the world.

Esther and Mordecai

In the days of the captivity of Israel and Judah there was a king; Ahasuerus and he made a great banquet seven days. There was drinking and making merry all of those days and on the seventh day, the king was merry with wine. He called for the queen to be brought before him and his guests, to show off her beauty to them. But the queen; Vashti was defiant and didn't obey the king's command, as this was a demand made under the influence of wine and arrogance. However, it was not wise to defy the king and especially while he was in the company of his guests. There was a suggestion made that Queen Vashti should never come again before the king and she should be replaced. Perhaps an awkward situation for the queen had become her demise and the point at which the rest of her life would be determined. Life can change in a moment and take a drastic new direction without warning, especially in a godless society. This, however, would be a necessary sacrifice as the people of Israel were in danger of total destruction. Afterward, the king's servants made a suggestion to have all of the beautiful women of the land to be brought before the king. The king could then choose for himself a new queen from among these fairest of the land. As you might expect, this pleased the king and he made the decree and signed it. So it was that the king's men set out over all of the provinces and gathered the most beautiful women and brought them to the palace to be prepped for the king.

Now in Shushan, there was a young woman by the Hebrew name of Hadassah also known as Esther. She had no parents and was raised by her cousin Mordecai. Providence would come to visit this young woman for a purpose greater than she could have ever imagined. Esther was very beautiful and was wise as well so she had the favor of God and God had chosen her to be His vessel.

Est 2:7-8 KJV And he brought up Hadassah, that is, Esther, his uncle's daughter: for she had neither father nor mother, and the maid was fair and beautiful; whom Mordecai, when her father and mother were dead, took for his own daughter. (8) So it came to pass, when the king's commandment and his decree was heard, and when many maidens were gathered together unto

Shushan the palace, to the custody of Hegai, that Esther was brought also unto the king's house, to the custody of Hegai, keeper of the women.

Now always when the favor of God is upon a person they are endowed with a countenance of light and are in the favor of people. There is something about the divine presence of God that stirs the heart and gives a peaceful desire to be close and results in admiration.

Est 2:9 KJV And the maiden pleased him, and she obtained kindness of him; and he speedily gave her her things for purification, with such things as belonged to her, and seven maidens, which were meet to be given her, out of the king's house: and he preferred her and her maids unto the best place of the house of the women.

Already Esther was given favor of the keeper because she stood out among all of the women. This should be true of a good Christian in that one stands out among the lost as possessing something unseen, that is desirable to the soul and finds favor in close communication. The Spirit of the Lord is the one that is absent in the heart of the lost and His attributes are only seen from a distance. When they see His attributes in you, they more often desire to know Him.

Esther possessed the qualities that were necessary for the purpose that she would soon fulfill. Now the Jews were in exile in the land and at the command of Mordecai, Esther never let it be known that she was a Jew. This turns out to be a very wise decision for the plan of God to be executed and she didn't even know it. The purification time of all of the women was twelve months and then the time had arrived that they would be presented before the king. Mordecai had been keeping informed of what would become of Esther as he very often sat at the gate. The city gates were a place of communication where information was transacted and legal matters were addressed and such as pertained to social affairs. As the time came for each woman to go before the king, they were presented with gifts and fine jewelry and could take whatever they desired with them. They then were taken to their dwelling in the palace where they would become part of the harem.

Est 2:15-17 KJV Now when the turn of Esther, the daughter of Abihail the uncle of Mordecai, who had taken her for his daughter, was come to go in unto the king, she required nothing but what Hegai the king's chamberlain, the keeper of the women, appointed. And Esther obtained favour in the sight of all them that looked upon her. (16) So Esther was taken unto king Ahasuerus into his house royal in the tenth month, which is the month Tebeth, in the seventh year of his reign. (17) And the king loved Esther above all the women, and she obtained grace and favour in his sight more than all the virgins; so that he set the royal crown upon her head, and made her queen instead of Vashti.

You see that Esther was not interested in the expensive gifts, but held to her friendship with the keeper. There are treasures that are more valuable than fine jewelry and gold that make one wealthy. This quality was beautiful in the sight of the others because her heart was for greater things. When you value God more than anything else, you become a witness for Him just by your presence. Now Esther has become the Queen and her life has taken a turn for greater days. Can you see how that God moves in these situations? His timing is perfect and His ways are past finding out.

Rom 11:33 KJV O the depth of the riches both of the wisdom and knowledge of God! how unsearchable are his judgments, and his ways past finding out!

Another piece of God's divine puzzle would be set in place so that the future would find Mordecai in the grace of the king. This is God's hand at work behind the scenes that will reveal His glory in the sight of the people.

Est 2:21-23 KJV In those days, while Mordecai sat in the king's gate, two of the king's chamberlains, Bigthan and Teresh, of those which kept the door, were wroth, and sought to lay hand on the king Ahasuerus. (22) And the thing was known to Mordecai, who told it unto Esther the queen; and Esther certified the king thereof in Mordecai's name. (23) And when inquisition was made of the matter, it was found out; therefore they were both hanged on a tree: and it was written in the book of the chronicles before the king.

Mordecai had saved the life of the king because of God's providence in that he was at the gate at the right time and was willing to protect the king. It is always better to do the right thing as God is aware of the very thoughts of our hearts. If we're willing to obey God, then we become active participants in the great plan of the ages that will culminate in the greatest kingdom of all time. Now there was a man by the name of Haman, that was set as the king's right-hand man and was given great authority over all the officials of the land; second only to the king. Haman was an Agagite, which means that he was a descendant of King Agag of the Amalekites. In the days of Saul, the first king of Israel; God; through the Prophet Samuel, had commanded that Saul utterly destroy all that pertained to the Amalekites, but Saul disobeyed God and didn't fulfill the command as he was told. Now we see how the actions of one man can affect the future. Haman hated the Jewish people and his heart was driven by his hatred to destroy the Jews. This is interesting in that God's original command was to wipe out the Amalekites, but because of the disobedience of Saul, Haman will now attempt to wipe out the Jews.

Est 3:2 KJV And all the king's servants, that were in the king's gate, bowed, and reverenced Haman: for the king had so commanded concerning him. But Mordecai bowed not, nor did him reverence.

Mordecai would become a thorn in Haman's flesh because of his defiance in not bowing to him. This would become a battle of wills which Haman could not win because God is in it. Haman's arrogance would become his enemy one day, but for now, it was his driving force. God can use even the worst attitude to fulfill His word and affect the outcome of any situation so that the glory is His.

Est 3:5-6 KJV And when Haman saw that Mordecai bowed not, nor did him reverence, then was Haman full of wrath. (6) And he thought scorn to lay hands on Mordecai alone; for they had shewed him the people of Mordecai: wherefore Haman sought to destroy all the Jews that were throughout the whole kingdom of Ahasuerus, even the people of Mordecai.

It seems that God has begun to stir up the heart of Haman to make his plans against the Jewish people so that God's plan will go forward. When God's time comes, He causes the elements of His plan to prosper in rapid succession. His timing is exact and even His enemies fall into place. God judges all and He will bring justice through one man's unjust actions. Haman will soon find out that the seeds of his actions will bring a great harvest of return to him.

Gal 6:7 KJV Be not deceived; God is not mocked: for whatsoever a man soweth, that shall he also reap.

Haman now begins to hatch his plan to destroy the Jewish people and the battle begins, not between

Mordecai and Haman, but between God and Haman. God's hand is at work here and everything that happens will be according to His plan.

Est 3:8-10 KJV And Haman said unto king Ahasuerus, There is a certain people scattered abroad and dispersed among the people in all the provinces of thy kingdom; and their laws are diverse from all people; neither keep they the king's laws: therefore it is not for the king's profit to suffer them. (9) If it please the king, let it be written that they may be destroyed: and I will pay ten thousand talents of silver to the hands of those that have the charge of the business, to bring it into the king's treasuries. (10) And the king took his ring from his hand, and gave it unto Haman the son of Hammedatha the Agagite, the Jews' enemy.

So now the gears are set in motion and Haman believes that he is in control, but God is directing Haman through his own arrogance and hatred. When a man defies the living God, he brings his own destruction by the evil that dwells in his own heart. His own words will be his demise and righteousness will prevail.

Mat 12:36-37 KJV But I say unto you, That every idle word that men shall speak, they shall give account thereof in the day of judgment. (37) For by thy words thou shalt be justified, and by thy words thou shalt be condemned.

As Haman condemns the Jewish people, he is building an airtight case against himself for when his time comes. Remember that a seed of bitterness will grow into a vine that will rise up and choke the life out of you. In this case, Haman's evil heart will be the door to freedom for God's people.

Est 3:13-14 KJV And the letters were sent by posts into all the king's provinces, to destroy, to kill, and to cause to perish, all Jews, both young and old, little children and women, in one day, even upon the thirteenth day of the twelfth month, which is the month Adar, and to take the spoil of them for a prey. (14) The copy of the writing for a commandment to be given in every province was published unto all people, that they should be ready against that day.

Now the decree has gone out and according to the laws of the Mede's and Persian's, the decree cannot be rescinded once the king has signed it. So the evil heart of Haman has condemned to death, every Jew in the land. On the specified day, everyone in every province has the right to kill every Jew and take their possessions and money. This is a heinous act of genocide against God's people, but God has already laid the groundwork for His success.

Psa 7:11-16 KJV God judgeth the righteous, and God is angry with the wicked every day. (12) If he turn not, he will whet his sword; he hath bent his bow, and made it ready. (13) He hath also prepared for him the instruments of death; he ordaineth his arrows against the persecutors.

(14) Behold, he travaileth with iniquity, and hath conceived mischief, and brought forth falsehood. (15) He made a pit, and digged it, and is fallen into the ditch which he made. (16) His mischief shall return upon his own head, and his violent dealing shall come down upon his own pate.

Haman is now in God's crosshairs, but God is just and He will act according to His righteous judgments because there is always hope when God is involved. However; Haman gives God the necessity for His judgment in this case, because of his hardened heart. There was much mourning in the land because of the decree and the Jews showed their brokenness by wearing sackcloth and sprinkling ashes on their heads. Mordecai did the same and sat at the gate where all could see.

Est 4:1-2 KJV When Mordecai perceived all that was done, Mordecai rent his clothes, and put on sackcloth with ashes, and went out into the midst of the city, and cried with a loud and a bitter cry; (2) And came even before the king's gate: for none might enter into the king's gate clothed with sackcloth.

Esther didn't know what Haman had done and sent a message to Mordecai to find out what was wrong. Mordecai sends the letter of the decree back to Esther and asks her to intervene and ask the king to stop this thing. But Esther knew that anyone that comes before the king without invitation would face death unless the king holds out the scepter to them. So Esther replied back to

Mordecai, this information.

Est 4:13-14 KJV Then Mordecai commanded to answer Esther, Think not with thyself that thou shalt escape in the king's house, more than all the Jews. (14) For if thou altogether holdest thy peace at this time, then shall there enlargement and deliverance arise to the Jews from another place; but thou and thy father's house shall be destroyed: and who knoweth whether thou art come to the kingdom for such a time as this?

The king didn't know that Esther was a Jew when he signed the decree, so now Esther was a target and the law could not be changed. Now Esther was faced with a dangerous choice and this is where faith in God is revealed from the heart. Esther's faith had to be greater than life itself in this moment of truth. Mordecai understood that this was Esther's destiny and that if she didn't seize this opportunity then God would use someone else and she might die anyway. Now is the time for that seed of greatness to sprout and take root.

Est 4:15-17 KJV Then Esther bade them return Mordecai this answer, (16) Go, gather together all the Jews that are present in Shushan, and fast ye for me, and neither eat nor drink three days, night or day: I also and my maidens will fast likewise; and so will I go in unto the king, which is not according to the law: and if I perish, I perish. (17) So Mordecai went his way, and did according to all that Esther had commanded him.

Esther now takes on a task greater than anything

that she has ever encountered and she will risk her life for her people. What kind of risks do we face in this world today? Integrity is the foundation of faith in that we must hold to our faith no matter what the circumstances. We can learn from Esther, the kind of determination that it takes to move the heart of a king.

So Esther puts on her royal apparel and takes the plunge and stands in the court of the king to see whether she will be received or die. This is a moment of truth and Esther's fate will be determined in an instant of time. But as providence would intervene; the king held out the golden scepter to her and she touched it. Today the King of glory has held out His scepter to us because in Christ; He has received us to Himself. This is a beautiful picture of the fact that we deserved death, but God has given us life.

So now Esther will plan a banquet for only three people; herself, the king and Haman. This will jumpstart Haman's arrogance because he is the only guest of the king and queen. Can you see how Haman's heart would be lifted up and how he might brag of his position to everyone? This will fulfill God's word as always God's word is in everything.

Pro 16:18 KJV Pride goeth before destruction, and an haughty spirit before a fall.

Haman now has been invited to the banquet and is high on his own conceit and he attends. The king asks Esther what her request was but she said that she would tell the king if they would attend another banquet the next day. When the banquet is over, Haman is exhilarated, but as he is headed home from the banquet, he encounters Mordecai that won't bow to him. But Haman is too charged to be concerned with that, so he makes his way home to brag about himself. In bragging; Haman expresses his disdain for Mordecai and his friends suggest that he make a fifty-foot tall gallows with which to hang Mordecai. So Haman soon orders the gallows to be built. Again God's providence would come to the king as he couldn't sleep so he ordered the books to be brought and he began to read. He found where that Mordecai had saved his life and there had been nothing done for his loyalty. The king asks who is in the court and they reply that Haman was there. Haman was coming to gain permission of the king to hang Mordecai on the gallows. This is no coincidence and God does have a sense of humor. Here's Haman coming to ask the king permission to kill the man that the king desires to reward. However; knowledge is power and Haman had no idea of this, but when the king asked him how a man's loyalty should be rewarded, Haman naturally thought he was the man.

Est 6:6-9 KJV So Haman came in. And the king said unto him, What shall be done unto the man whom the king delighteth to honour? Now Haman thought in his heart, To whom would the king delight to do honour more than to myself?

(7) And Haman answered the king, For the man whom the king delighteth to honour, (8) Let the royal apparel be brought which the king useth to wear, and the horse that the king rideth upon, and the crown royal which is set upon his head: (9) And let this apparel and horse be delivered to the hand of one of the king's most noble princes, that they may array the man withal whom the king delighteth to honour, and bring him on horseback through the street of the city, and proclaim before him, Thus shall it be done to the man whom the king delighteth to honour.

Haman is now so exalted within himself that it will be great fall when he hears who will be receiving this honor. When you are focused on yourself, it is difficult for you to see God's purpose and you will be caught off guard in a time when you least expect it.

Est 6:10 KJV Then the king said to Haman, Make haste, and take the apparel and the horse, as thou hast said, and do even so to Mordecai the Jew, that sitteth at the king's gate: let nothing fail of all that thou hast spoken.

You can't go against God and win, no matter how good that you think you are, God searches the hearts of people and He knows your intentions. After Haman's humiliation at Mordecai's reward, he naturally ends up at home complaining to his wife. Then the messenger delivers the word that Haman is to come to the banquet again this day. Again as God's providence would have it, this is the hour of the vengeance of God and Haman's time has run out. Esther reveals that she is, in fact, a Jew and Haman has run a campaign to destroy the Jews. The king's fury is kindled at this and he orders Haman and his ten sons to be hanged on the gallows that were built for Mordecai. God had given Haman ample time to repent, but Haman's hatred kept him chained to destruction. The king gave Mordecai the position that Haman held and the king's ring, so the tables have turned and justice has prevailed. The decree couldn't be rescinded, so the king gave Mordecai the authority to make another decree so that the Jewish people could retaliate.

Est 8:10-11 KJV And he wrote in the king Ahasuerus' name, and sealed it with the king's ring, and sent letters by posts on horseback, and riders on mules, camels, and young dromedaries: (11) Wherein the king granted the Jews which were in every city to gather themselves together, and to stand for their life, to destroy, to slay, and to cause to perish, all the power of the people and province that would assault them, both little ones and women, and to take the spoil of them for a prey,

When the time came there was an uprising, but the Jews gained the victory over their enemies. These were the ones that were willing to slay them and there were many that sided with the Jewish people. So in this skirmish; God not only slew Haman, but He also defeated all of their enemies from within the kingdom. This time is celebrated even today and is called the Feast of Purim because the Jews were saved from annihilation. See how that God directs the destiny of His people? When evil rises up to destroy utterly the passion of God; He empowers them to stand strong and prevail. You may have a situation that seems impossible to you, but God will empower you to see it through and prevail in the end. Here are yet two more lights that have proven that God is on the throne and has given the seed of greatness into His people.

Job

Sometimes we wonder; "how will I ever get through this?" When problems arise, they are never met with complete joy. I'm not a big fan of trouble and most of the time, I try to avoid it. However, if we never had to experience struggle, then how would we ever become stronger? If there were no problems in this life, we might never know the joy of victory or the value of peace. Again, if there were no struggles in this life, then we would never know the kind of love that comes with sacrificing for others to share their pain. We would not experience true love because there wouldn't be the need for that sacrifice and a faithful promise. The bad times always make the good times much brighter. Each of us is fashioned like fine jewelry or a master painting by the struggles that we endure in this life. Like a fingerprint, there are no two people that are the same. Our struggles are like the fire that tempers the steel and refines the gold. Each time we endure a trial to the end, we come out of it more than we were before. Some people must endure much more than others and it is the way that they turn their heart that determines the reward. The true lights in this world are the ones that grow through their pain and resist a bitter attitude. The more that we endure with humility, the more beautiful the painting becomes, and greater is the outcome because the least shall be the greatest.

Jas 1:2-4 KJV My brethren, count it all joy when ye fall into divers temptations; (3) Knowing this, that the trying of your faith worketh patience. (4) But let patience have her perfect work, that ye may be perfect and entire, wanting nothing.

A very long time ago there was a man named Job that lived in the land of Uz. Job was very wealthy and was blessed of the Lord and was a righteous man in all of his ways. He hated evil and lived a life of service to God. This was a problem for Satan because God was pleased with Job and He was vocal about it when Satan presented himself before God.

Job 1:6-8 KJV Now there was a day when the sons of God came to present themselves before the LORD, and Satan came also among them. (7) And the LORD said unto Satan, Whence comest thou? Then Satan answered the LORD, and said,

From going to and fro in the earth, and from walking up and down in it. (8) And the LORD said unto Satan, Hast thou considered my servant Job, that there is none like him in the earth, a perfect and an upright man, one that feareth God, and escheweth evil?

Now, these words are a proof that God is interested in our walk as His people. He is the Creator of the universe and yet He is concerned about us individually. No matter what you have done or what you may be facing today; God is watching and guiding as you experience life. Job knew that it was the blessing of God that made him strong and wealthy. He understood the importance of following God's law and living according to His will. When a man lives of his own will and does his own thing; he is against the will of God and against the blessings that are a result of doing God's will. However, in Job's case, there were circumstances that were far beyond Job's control.

Job 1:9-12 KJV Then Satan answered the LORD, and said, Doth Job fear God for nought? (10) Hast not thou made an hedge about him, and about his house, and about all that he hath on every side? thou hast blessed the work of his hands, and his substance is increased in the land. (11) But put forth thine hand now, and touch all that he hath, and he will curse thee to thy face. (12) And the LORD said unto Satan, Behold, all that he hath is in thy power; only upon himself put not forth thine hand. So Satan went forth from the presence of the LORD.

Now Satan began a campaign of destroying all that Job possessed in the world. As if that was not enough, Satan is a murderer; he also killed Job's children. So now Job is left with no possessions and no children. When we look at Job's situation, there is nothing that can compare to his completely devastated existence. Personally, I can't comprehend the deep and despairing emotional pain that Job must have felt through this. There is a propensity in the human nature to nurture a seed of bitterness in hard times that will control the attitude and strike out against God. Satan was well aware of this and was beating hard against Job's life to bring this about. Job, however, was steadfast in his trusting God and maintained his integrity.

Job 1:20-22 KJV Then Job arose, and rent his mantle, and shaved his head, and fell down upon the ground, and worshipped, (21) And said, Naked came I out of my mother's womb, and naked shall I return thither: the LORD gave, and the LORD hath taken away; blessed be the name of the LORD. (22) In all this Job sinned not, nor charged God foolishly.

I'm not sure that there are many of us, that if we received such bump in the road of life, could maintain as did Job. He lost everything in a very short period of time and became a sore sight, but he knew that God had provided these things and was privileged to take them away if He pleased. Job knew the source of true life and blessing and these are by the hand of God. When you experience a trial, it may be that there is something in your life that needs to be worked out, so that you can advance. No one deserves the good things in this life because we have all sinned and broken covenant with our Maker. God has given His mercy and grace because He loves us beyond our inadequacies. As you can see by Job's story; this is not God that has devastated Job's life. Satan has to receive permission to cause havoc in someone's life, but it was Satan that did this thing to Job. Even though Job was a righteous man, that didn't mean that there would never be trouble in his life. Becoming a Christian doesn't guarantee a life without problems and they do happen, but we have hope in Christ. A person will make choices in this life and evil is always ready to enter when a door is open by a bad decision.

Gal 6:7-9 KJV Be not deceived; God is not mocked: for whatsoever a man soweth, that shall he also reap. (8) For he that soweth to his flesh shall of the flesh reap corruption; but he that soweth to the Spirit shall of the Spirit reap life everlasting. (9) And let us not be weary in well doing: for in due season we shall reap, if we faint not.

Again here is the patience of Job that we faint not and stand fast no matter what the situation. As we have seen; Job maintained his integrity after he lost everything, so now Satan seeks to touch Job's flesh with his evil.

Job 2:3-7 KJV And the LORD said unto Satan, Hast thou considered my servant Job, that there is none like him in the earth, a perfect and an upright man, one that feareth God, and escheweth evil? and still he holdeth fast his integrity, although thou movedst me against him, to destroy him without cause. (4) And Satan answered the LORD, and said, Skin for skin, yea, all that a man hath will he give for his life. (5) But put forth thine hand now, and touch his bone and his flesh, and he will curse thee to thy face. (6) And the LORD said unto Satan, Behold, he is in thine hand; but save his life. (7) So went Satan forth from the presence of the LORD, and smote Job with sore boils from the sole of his foot unto his crown.

Now Job faces agony in the flesh with painful boils so much that he has to scrape them with a piece of broken pottery. Now Job is really a sight to behold; he goes from a very wealthy and influential member of society to a badly scarred beggar sitting in the ashes of shame and disgust. How agonizing and depressing a life to endure for a man that was once looked at as great. Greatness is not the outward man that is seen by the world but is the inner man that only God can see. God is the one that will reveal your true heart when the time comes. Job is flesh as are the rest of us but Job has a heart for God; how is your heart towards God especially in times of trouble? Job's wife gives him bad advice which is common in this world:

Job 2:9-10 KJV Then said his wife unto him, Dost thou still retain thine integrity? curse God, and die. (10) But he said unto her, Thou speakest as one of the foolish women speaketh. What? shall we receive good at the hand of God, and shall we not receive evil? In all this did not Job sin with his lips.

Have you ever considered this that Job said? Shall we receive good from God and not the bad? I sure don't like the bad stuff, but in this life, there has to be resistance to good or we could never grow stronger. Think about this; when we resist evil and do good in bad times, we are showing God how much we believe Him and love Him. We have to make a concerted effort to be in God's will and favor. This involves faith and that is the thing that pleases God.

Now Job had three friends that came to console him and at first, they remained silent in his presence. But when they began to speak, they had nothing encouraging to say. Job knew that he didn't sin that he should reap this harvest of destruction, but that it came upon him for reasons known only to God. But these friends believed that there had to be a reason for his suffering that was originated in sin. What did Job do wrong to receive such a harsh judgment? But the reality of this is just what Job asked: "shall we receive good from God and not bad?" After arguing for a time

Job begins to speak words that all of us might feel if we were in his situation. He curses the day that he was born and wishes that he never existed. Doesn't that sound like us when we are in despair? I don't believe that any of us are made of steel, not even Job and he breaks down, but he never does curse God. Can any of us say that we never had harsh words towards God in our deepest trials? Perhaps some can, but when we see the integrity of Job, we have something to strive for and a hope that resides in faith.

There came a day when God Himself showed up in a whirlwind. He began asking Job questions of a sort that he couldn't answer but gave him a new perspective.

Job 38:1-4 KJV Then the LORD answered Job out of the whirlwind, and said, (2) Who is this that darkeneth counsel by words without knowledge? (3) Gird up now thy loins like a man; for I will demand of thee, and answer thou me. (4) Where wast thou when I laid the foundations of the earth? declare, if thou hast understanding.

I feel for Job in this because he was blindsided without warning and was left pondering his very existence. But God never does a thing without a purpose. If He allows evil to touch your life then there will be a good result if you can endure. In Job's case, God was never displeased with him even though His questions seem to be harsh. When I think about what God has done for us in satisfying the penalty for sin in His only begotten

Son; I know that God loves us all. As a good Father, God directs Job's attention to his lack of understanding and the faith that it takes to just believe Him. God's chiding of Job serves to encourage him and us as well that we don't know everything, but that God loves us more than we know. Now God gives rebuke to Job's friends:

Job 42:7-8 KJV And it was so, that after the LORD had spoken these words unto Job, the LORD said to Eliphaz the Temanite, My wrath is kindled against thee, and against thy two friends: for ye have not spoken of me the thing that is right, as my servant Job hath. (8) Therefore take unto you now seven bullocks and seven rams, and go to my servant Job, and offer up for yourselves a burnt offering; and my servant Job shall pray for you: for him will I accept: lest I deal with you after your folly, in that ye have not spoken of me the thing which is right, like my servant Job.

After these things; God restored to Job twice as much as he had before and gave him ten more children to replace the ten that died. So now he has twenty children; ten with him and ten in paradise. So Job was greater after his trial than he was before. Another light on the pathway of God's creative journey for us to get to His perfect will and become great lights that God has ordained for us.

Daniel and his friends

As a young boy sleeps, the sun begins to illuminate the horizon and birds are chirping their songs to each other. The sound of people moving about fills the air as they rise to greet the morning sun and prepare for another day. Suddenly the blissful peace is interrupted as the sounds of shofars begin blasting away their warnings into the morning air. There comes a sound just outside the big wooden gates on the wall of the city and suddenly a loud bang that shakes the ground. The boy is startled awake and begins to look around and people are running back and forth in a panic. Again another bang and shouts ring out from all over the city. The boy's mother runs to him commanding him to run and to hide at the synagogue. Another bang overpowers the noise of scurrying and then a crash and the voices of men yelling and horse hooves pounding the ground like an earthquake. As the boy runs through the street the smell of smoke fills his nostrils as fires begin appearing everywhere. As he scans the landscape he sees men falling to the ground with arrows protruding from their bodies. He sees strange men with swords slashing the bodies of everyone in their paths. Smoke begins filling the air and the boy can no longer see what is happening. Nebuchadnezzar and his armies had broken through and sacked the city and taken those that were alive captive and carried them off to Babylon.

Now Nebuchadnezzar commanded that the brightest and well favored young people be brought to the palace.

Dan 1:3-4 KJV And the king spake unto Ashpenaz the master of his eunuchs, that he should bring certain of the children of Israel, and of the king's seed, and of the princes; (4) Children in whom was no blemish, but well favoured, and skilful in all wisdom, and cunning in knowledge, and understanding science, and such as had ability in them to stand in the king's palace, and whom they might teach the learning and the tongue of the Chaldeans.

As Moses the servant of God was raised up in the learning and tongue of Egypt; so a young boy by the name of Daniel would be raised up in the learning and tongue of Babylon. These young men were taken away from their homeland and familiar surroundings into a world of stark contrast to what they knew. Babylon had all kinds of gods but these knew only of the one true and living God. Daniel was a believer and his faith was the important aspect of his existence, no matter what life would bring. So when the king had ordered that they should be given the best food from the king's pantries, it was Daniel that would make a request for a different kind of food. Now the food that the king provided would, to a Jew be a defilement according to his faith. Daniel requested that they should be given vegetables to eat, but the man that was given charge of them feared what the king would do if they were not as healthy as the others. But Daniel asked if they could be proven for ten days and then see if they were not as healthy as the others, so he obliged them. So after ten days they compared the youth and found Daniel and those with him that ate the vegetables were fatter and healthier than those that ate the king's food. From then on they gave them vegetables to eat. Daniel's faith was tested and prevailed in a serious situation. This would begin to affect the perspective of those that observed him. We will be confronted with issues that try our faith in this life, but if we truly believe God then we should stand on the inerrancy of His word and not conform to the world. This is one way that people will remember us and will stand as a testimony in the future of God's perfect will. If you are a believer then you will be different than the unbelievers and become a standard for what is right. Daniel was a representative of God's people and he took his stand for that which was right according to their faith. From his youth, Daniel made an impression because he was not afraid of them as his trust was in God as with his three friends.

Dan 1:17-20 KJV As for these four children, God gave them knowledge and skill in all learning and wisdom: and Daniel had understanding in all visions and dreams. (18) Now at the end of the days that the king had said he should bring them in, then the prince of the eunuchs brought them in before Nebuchadnezzar. (19) And the king communed with them; and among them all was found none like Daniel, Hananiah, Mishael, and Azariah: therefore stood they before the king. (20) And in all matters of wisdom and understanding, that the king enquired of them, he found them ten times better than all the magicians and astrologers that were in all his realm.

These four boys would stand out because God was with them and if God is for you, evil cannot hinder your progress in this world. Although they were given favor with God and man, there would be opposition from Satan in many ways. When you walk close to God, your light will shine and the enemy will see it and he doesn't like the light because his domain is darkness.

One night the king had a dream and was troubled

and so he called for all of the magicians and astrologers and the sorcerers to show him his dream. There was one problem with this and that was that the king forgot the dream. Now the real test came and this one would separate the true prophet from the hypocrites. When the impossible confronts you, only God can prevail. The king threatened to destroy every one of them if they could not tell him the dream.

Dan 2:8-10 KJV The king answered and said, I know of certainty that ye would gain the time, because ye see the thing is gone from me. (9) But if ye will not make known unto me the dream, there is but one decree for you: for ye have prepared lying and corrupt words to speak before me, till the time be changed: therefore tell me the dream, and I shall know that ye can shew me the interpretation thereof. (10) The Chaldeans answered before the king, and said, There is not a man upon the earth that can shew the king's matter: therefore there is no king, lord, nor ruler, that asked such things at any magician, or astrologer, or Chaldean.

This is the way of the world in that there are limitations on the wicked and they say that there is not a man that can tell the king his dream. Now, this is the setup so that the king can see that God is greater than any of the wisest men and that there are no other gods that can compare. So the king orders the death of all the wise men and the sorcerers and magicians. Now when they come to take Daniel and his friends, this is a surprise to them and Daniel asks for some time to pray so that he may tell the king his dream. You see, Daniel knew the source of all wisdom in the universe and his faith again would get him through this. God's people stand in the way of evil and in this; Satan would have destroyed the king's source of wisdom. Daniel was God's man and this would have removed him from the path of Satan's destructive ways. But Daniel sought God's wisdom and he prayed and God gave him the answer. This was life or death and the timing was last minute, so Daniel was tested to the very limit. Daniel would stop the hand of darkness as God's people do and he would tell the king, his dream. What the other men saw as impossible was the entry point for the power of God and Daniel was the conduit.

Dan 2:19-23 KJV Then was the secret revealed unto Daniel in a night vision. Then Daniel blessed the God of heaven. (20) Daniel answered and said, Blessed be the name of God for ever and ever: for wisdom and might are his: (21) And he changeth the times and the seasons: he removeth kings, and setteth up kings: he giveth wisdom unto the wise, and knowledge to them that know understanding: (22) He revealeth the deep and secret things: he knoweth what is in the darkness, and the light dwelleth with him. (23) I thank thee, and praise thee, O thou God of my fathers, who hast given me wisdom and might, and hast made known unto me now what we desired of thee: for thou hast now made known unto us the king's matter.

Only the true and living God can overcome the impossible because He is the Creator. If you have received Jesus Christ then are you an over comer of the impossible, by His blood and authority in the universe.

Daniel and these three friends were true believers and their faith was rewarded and a greater purpose was achieved.

Dan 2:27-29 KJV Daniel answered in the presence of the king, and said, The secret which the king hath demanded cannot the wise men, the astrologers, the magicians, the soothsayers, shew unto the king; (28) But there is a God in heaven that revealeth secrets, and maketh known to the king Nebuchadnezzar what shall be in the latter days. Thy dream, and the visions of thy head upon thy bed, are these; (29) As for thee, O king, thy thoughts came into thy mind upon thy bed, what should come to pass hereafter: and he that revealeth secrets maketh known to thee what shall come to pass.

Daniel proceeds to tell the king all of his dream and the interpretation. The king was so impressed at the fact that Daniel could tell him his dream and then interpret the dream that he fell on his face and worshipped Daniel. Can you see this? This was the king and he gives obeisance to a common man because of his God. But Daniel was uncommon by his faith in God and so the impossible manifested before the king. This is the providence of God and He will turn the heart of a king to see all of the truth eventually. The king promoted Daniel and this is God's will; it doesn't matter what the situation; God will have His people in the right places:

Dan 2:47-49 KJV The king answered unto Daniel, and said, Of a truth it is, that your God is a God of gods, and a Lord of kings, and a revealer of secrets, seeing thou couldest reveal this secret. (48) Then the king made Daniel a great man, and gave him many great gifts, and made him ruler over the whole province of Babylon, and chief of the governors over all the wise men of Babylon. (49) Then Daniel requested of the king, and he set Shadrach, Meshach, and Abednego, over the affairs of the province of Babylon: but Daniel sat in the gate of the king.

Satan tried to destroy the plan of God, but he got blindsided by the faith of God's people. It may seem to be terrible to be in captivity to another nation, but with God, there can be greatness even under oppressive rule.

2Co 3:17 KJV Now the Lord is that Spirit: and where the Spirit of the Lord is, there is liberty.

If you believe the words of God and these great moments in history, then you can experience the impossible, because faith in God trumps the impossible in any situation.

Though Nebuchadnezzar was impressed by the God of Daniel, he still was not converted. He had a giant statue built:

Dan 3:1 KJV Nebuchadnezzar the king made an image of gold, whose height was threescore cubits, and the breadth thereof six cubits: he set it up in the plain of Dura, in the province of Babylon.

The king summoned all of the leaders of the land to come together to dedicate the statue and the command went out that at the sound of the musical instruments, everyone should bow down to the statue. Shadrach, Meshach, and Abednego were officials and were present at the dedication. Again the faith of the faithful would be tested as the punishment for failure to bow was the fiery furnace. Now the music began and all across the area, people got down on their knees and began to worship the statue. Three men remained standing and did not bow to the statue; this was a decision in a matter of life and death. The faith of these men and their reverence for God was greater than the heinous fiery punishment that awaited them. There are places in the earth today that faith in Jesus Christ is a death sentence and many people die for the name of Jesus. Satan has no mercy and his will is to steal, to kill and to destroy all that pertains to God. But when you take a stand against evil, you hinder the plan of the evil one. In the case of Shadrach, Meshach, and Abednego; there is a providential reason for the outcome of their resistance to this idolatry. God has a plan and Satan is powerless to stop it from being fulfilled.

The king is warned of these men that didn't bow and he becomes furious:

Dan 3:12-13 KJV There are certain Jews whom thou hast set over the affairs of the province of Babylon, Shadrach, Meshach, and Abednego; these men, O king, have not regarded thee: they serve not thy gods, nor worship the golden image which thou hast set up. (13) Then Nebuchadnezzar in his rage and fury commanded to bring Shadrach, Meshach, and Abednego. Then they brought these men before the king.

This is the moment of truth and these men will be given one more chance, but they are steadfast in their faith and respect for God. They can either obey the king and bow or obey God and face certain death. These men had faith like Job and Job said it right:

Job 13:14-16 KJV Wherefore do I take my flesh in my teeth, and put my life in mine hand? (15) Though he slay me, yet will I trust in him: but I will maintain mine own ways before him. (16) He also shall be my salvation: for an hypocrite shall not come before him.

Even if it is God's will that they die, then die they will do because salvation is of God and not of man.

Dan 3:16-18 KJV Shadrach, Meshach, and Abednego, answered and said to the king, O Nebuchadnezzar, we are not careful to answer thee in this matter. (17) If it be so, our God whom we serve is able to deliver us from the burning fiery furnace, and he will deliver us out of thine hand, O king. (18) But if not, be it known unto thee, O king, that we will not serve thy gods, nor worship the golden image which thou hast set up.

These men show true courage in the face of adversity and to serve God is a greater purpose than life itself. There is no room for complacency in a dying world of sinful deeds. How would you react if given the same choice? Could we know in advance how we would answer such a situation? If we are believers and faithful to God, then there should be no question as to what we would answer. Nebuchadnezzar was angered so much that he ordered that the furnace should be heated ten times hotter than normal insomuch that the soldiers who threw them in were themselves burned up. Now talk about an impossible situation, these men were cast to their death or so it seemed, but they served the true and living God. Now comes God's providence because the king saw four men in the fire and they were walking around in the midst of the fire. The king had forgotten his anger as he was amazed at what he was seeing. One thing that I might interject here is the fact that these men were no longer bound, but were loosed from their bonds. Perhaps the fire had burned the ropes from them as the power of God was their protection from the heat. Sometimes when we are in the midst of a trial, God has a purpose for it, in that it removes some hindrance that we have not overcome. His supernatural power is our protection in the heat of the trial and we can come out of it much more than we were before.

Dan 3:25-26 KJV He answered and said, Lo, I see four men loose, walking in the midst of the fire, and they have no hurt; and the form of the fourth is like the Son of God. (26) Then Nebuchadnezzar came near to the mouth of the burning fiery furnace, and spake, and said, Shadrach, Meshach, and Abednego, ye servants of the most high God, come forth, and come hither. Then Shadrach, Meshach, and Abednego, came forth of the midst of the fire.

We might ask "who was that fourth man?" I believe that this is the same man that shows up throughout the Old Testament and His form is like the Son of God. The New Testament is the revelation of Him and He is the Son of the Living God; Jesus Christ. God is planting seeds in the heart of the king as can be seen by his words "*ye servants of the most high God*". There is no god but our God in the universe because all others that call themselves god were created by God. Nebuchadnezzar is beginning to see the light as all of these supernatural events overpower any of the lies of the evil one. So these men come forth out of the super-heated fire and had no smell of smoke on them. Faith in God has prevailed and people were exposed to the real power of God and so in the judgment, there will be no excuse for those that still rejected Him. How is your faith today? Would hard time turn you away from God or will you trust Him all the more?

Dan 3:28-30 KJV Then Nebuchadnezzar spake, and said, Blessed be the God of Shadrach, Meshach, and Abednego, who hath sent his angel, and delivered his servants that trusted in him, and have changed the king's word, and yielded their bodies, that they might not serve nor worship any god, except their own God. (29) Therefore I make a decree, That every people, nation, and language, which speak any thing amiss against the God of Shadrach, Meshach, and Abednego, shall be cut in pieces, and their houses shall be made a dunghill: because there is no other God that can deliver after this sort. (30) Then the king promoted Shadrach, Meshach, and Abednego, in the province of Babylon.

The outcome of this fiery trial has brought to these men a promotion for their obedience to God and has exalted God in the heart of the king and before the people. Next time that you are faced with a dilemma concerning your faith in God, remember that these were facing death, but God delivered them. He didn't deliver them out of the fire, but from within the fire as He was with them in their trial. The fire had no more effect on them but that their faith was proven greater than the trial. They came out of their trial better than they were before and that is the purpose for the trials.

Jas 1:2-4 KJV My brethren, count it all joy when ye fall into divers temptations; (3) Knowing this, that the trying of your faith worketh patience.

(4) But let patience have her perfect work, that ye may be perfect and entire, wanting nothing.

Look beyond your trial and strive for the mastery that in the end of it you will have much more to offer to the world when it's over. If you will grow in your fiery trial, then your life will testify of God's power and grace and He will be exalted. There is no greater sense of purpose than to have suffered for the glory of God.

Now there came a day in that Nebuchadnezzar had another dream and again he called for the wise men, astrologers, and sorcerers to interpret the dream and last of all; Daniel came in and listened to the dream. The dream was not a good one and Daniel it says was troubled and for an hour he was pondering the dream. The king pressed Daniel for the interpretation and Daniel said that the dream was for his enemies. Nebuchadnezzar would be given the heart of a beast and would eat grass and live like an animal for seven years. The office of the king would be given over to whoever the Lord would choose, however, this was not permanent. There would come a day when Nebuchadnezzar would be restored to his throne, but none the less there was trouble on the horizon.

Dan 4:28-31 KJV All this came upon the king Nebuchadnezzar. (29) At the end of twelve months he walked in the palace of the kingdom of Babylon. (30) The king spake, and said, Is not this great Babylon, that I have built for the house of the kingdom by the might of my power, and for the honour of my majesty? (31) While the word was in the king's mouth, there fell a voice from heaven, saying, O king Nebuchadnezzar, to thee it is spoken; The kingdom is departed from thee.

The minute that Nebuchadnezzar exalted himself and boasted of his achievements without giving glory to God; it began.

Pro 16:18 KJV Pride goeth before destruction, and an haughty spirit before a fall.

When pride takes over it turns away from God and will lead you astray, eventually, you will fall. In this case, Nebuchadnezzar was in God's sight for conversion. God looks on the heart and Nebuchadnezzar, even though he was proud and an idolater, had good in himself. He showed respect for God and those that serve Him. God has greater things for this man and somewhere in the spectrum of eternity, there is a place for him. Know this, that God had placed Daniel in his life, so by this, we know that God is working on him. God will put you into the life of another so that your faith can affect them for the good. Always be obedient to God and He will make you an inspiration to others. Now Nebuchadnezzar became like an animal for seven years and he did eat grass. His fingernails grew long like claws and his hair matted like the feathers of a bird. Seven years he was out of his mind and had no capacity to reason for himself let alone rule a kingdom. But as the prophet told him; he would be restored to his throne. That day came when he became right in his mind again and was restored. Nebuchadnezzar had seen the light and he wrote a decree and these words are the only words in God's book that were penned by the hand of a Gentile.

Dan 4:34-37 KJV And at the end of the days I Nebuchadnezzar lifted up mine eyes unto heaven, and mine understanding returned unto me, and I blessed the most High, and I praised and honoured him that liveth for ever, whose dominion is an everlasting dominion, and his kingdom is from generation to generation: (35) And all the inhabitants of the earth are reputed as nothing: and he doeth according to his will in the army of heaven, and among the inhabitants of the earth: and none can stay his hand, or say unto him, What doest thou? (36) At the same time my reason returned unto me; and for the glory of my kingdom, mine honour and brightness returned unto me; and my counsellors and my lords sought unto me; and I was established in my kingdom, and excellent majesty was added unto me. (37) Now I Nebuchadnezzar praise and extol and honour the King of heaven, all whose works are truth, and his ways judgment: and those that walk in pride he is able to abase.

Reading these words we can see that obviously, Nebuchadnezzar had been changed in his heart and humbled by God. God's grace is powerful to overcome pride and to give wisdom where it once had lacked. Daniel and his friends, by their steadfast faithfulness to God, had inspired the king, thus making him open to God's word.

After the time of Nebuchadnezzar had past and a new regime had taken over Babylon; the Medes and the Persians, Daniel faced another test. You see, Daniel was in the favor of this ruler as well because of God's favor upon him. Darius was his name and he loved Daniel.

Dan 6:3 KJV Then this Daniel was preferred above the presidents and princes, because an excellent spirit was in him; and the king thought to set him over the whole realm.

This caused a spirit of envy and jealousy to rise up in the hearts of wicked men and so they sought after opportunity to do him harm. They watched him closely to find anything that they could use against him.

Dan 6:4 KJV Then the presidents and princes sought to find occasion against Daniel concerning the kingdom; but they could find none occasion nor fault; forasmuch as he was faithful, neither was there any error or fault found in him.

They couldn't find anything that he did wrong and that is true integrity. This is how we should be; when the enemy wants to destroy us, he should have trouble in this area. Now since they couldn't find anything wrong, they hatched a plan to change the law to make Daniels faith become his downfall. They wrote a decree that if anyone would pray to any god or man except for the king for the next thirty days, that he should be thrown into the den of lions. They did this because they saw that Daniel prayed three times a day. These are the rulers of the provinces, they are set over the land and trusted to rule wisely and justly. These men are allowing sin to rule in their lives and thus they affect the world around them adversely. These will stand before the Judge at that day and answer for this that they did to Daniel. God is just and fair and He will judge the sins of people from the beginning to the end.

Darius had signed this decree and now it couldn't be rescinded so Daniel's fate had been determined. I think that had Darius been in mind of Daniel, he would have never signed the decree. But now they could arrest Daniel for praying as he always did and this they proceeded to do.

Dan 6:13-14 KJV Then answered they and said before the king, That Daniel, which is of the children of the captivity of Judah, regardeth not thee, O king, nor the decree that thou hast signed, but maketh his petition three times a day. (14) Then the king, when he heard these words, was sore displeased with himself, and set his heart on Daniel to deliver him: and he laboured till the going down of the sun to deliver him.

He was trying to find a loophole to get Daniel out of this mess because he loved Daniel. These evil men had deceived the king and now his hands were tied, but God had a hand in this as His providence would prevail. Whatever you do, don't harbor sin and evil in your heart because God's righteousness will always win in the end. Darius couldn't find a loophole so he had to allow them to cast Daniel into the lion's den. The king was sleepless all night and worried about Daniel so when morning had come, he went directly to check on Daniel.

Dan 6:19-22 KJV Then the king arose very early in the morning, and went in haste unto the den of lions. (20) And when he came to the den, he cried with a lamentable voice unto Daniel: and the king spake and said to Daniel, O Daniel, servant of the living God, is thy God, whom thou servest continually, able to deliver thee from the lions? (21) Then said Daniel unto the king, O king, live for ever. (22) My God hath sent his angel, and hath shut the lions' mouths, that they have not hurt me: forasmuch as before him innocency was found in me; and also before thee, O king, have I done no hurt.

What a great witness to the world that God can stay the lion's mouth in whatever situation that you are in. Daniel prevails as did his friends that were thrown into the fiery furnace because God was with him. Now that Daniel was spared from the wrath of his enemies, it was time for justice to be done.

Dan 6:24 KJV And the king commanded, and they brought those men which had accused Daniel, and they cast them into the den of lions, them, their children, and their wives; and the lions had the mastery of them, and brake all their bones in pieces or ever they came at the bottom of the den.

As I said before; whatever you do, don't harbor sin and evil in your heart, because God's righteousness will prevail. Not only did the man of God escape unharmed, but his enemies were destroyed and everyone that was connected to them. God will deal with your enemies, so pray for them that their heart will change and they will be spared a fate of destruction. Here we have more bright lights on God's pathway that shine brightly along the way for us to see.

Paul and his conversion

All of Jesus' disciples walked with Jesus and had intimate knowledge of His personality and were His friends. They are the witnesses to His life and ministry up to and beyond His death, burial and resurrection. However there was another man that was divinely chosen to carry the gospel of Jesus into the world, but he had no idea of his true calling. Paul whose name is Saul early on in the book of Acts was a proud Pharisee and was the up and coming leader in the Jewish community. He had a pedigree so to speak as he was everything a great Jew was supposed to be and then some. Saul had a vision and a zeal for the word of God and this "way" was in his way. He saw the Christian faith as a heresy to Judaism and was bent on removing it from existence. He had much clout with the rulers of the community and thus was their great asset in overcoming all heresies concerning the faith. God cannot use a proud person because their hearts are set on their own conception of who He is and His attributes. Since God is beyond our ability to understand; pride closes the door to learning. If we think that we understand God, then we begin to place Him in a mental box, which is impossible to do.

Isa 55:7-9 KJV Let the wicked forsake his way, and the unrighteous man his thoughts: and let him return unto the LORD, and he will have mercy upon him; and to our God, for he will abundantly pardon. (8) For my thoughts are not your thoughts, neither are your ways my ways, saith the LORD. (9) For as the heavens are higher than the earth, so are my ways higher than your ways, and my thoughts than your thoughts.

Do you think that you understand Him today? When we are a million years into eternity, we will still have only a minute realization as to His greatness and divine existence. I don't think that we have the capability to know Him completely. Saul had an obstacle that needed to be removed before he could see the truth. Paul is introduced to us in chapter seven of the book of Acts and is demonstrating his disdain for the concept of this "way". Stephen a spirit filled man of God had just given a message that provoked the Jews to anger:

Act 7:55-58 KJV But he, being full of the Holy Ghost, looked up stedfastly into heaven, and saw the glory of God, and Jesus standing on the right hand of God, (56) And said, Behold, I see the heavens opened, and the Son of man standing on the right hand of God. (57) Then they cried out with a loud voice, and stopped their ears, and ran upon him with one accord, (58) And cast him out of the city, and stoned him: and the witnesses laid down their clothes at a young man's feet, whose name was Saul.

This man watched as Stephen was stoned to death and he had the authority to stop it from happening. But his zeal for the scriptures and traditions of his faith gave him a disdain for anything that he didn't understand.

Act 8:1-3 KJV And Saul was consenting unto his death. And at that time there was a great persecution against the church which was at Jerusalem; and they were all scattered abroad throughout the regions of Judaea and Samaria, except the apostles. (2) And devout men carried Stephen to his burial, and made great lamentation over him. (3) As for Saul, he made havock of the church, entering into every house, and haling men and women committed them to prison.

As Saul was fired up to go and imprison any people of the "way", he found his destiny on the road to Damascus in his search to find and destroy this that he saw as heirecy.

Act 9:1-6 KJV And Saul, yet breathing out threatenings and slaughter against the disciples of the Lord, went unto the high priest, (2) And desired of him letters to Damascus to the synagogues, that if he found any of this way, whether they were men or women, he might bring them bound unto Jerusalem. (3) And as he journeyed, he came near Damascus: and suddenly there shined round about him a light from heaven: (4) And he fell to the earth, and heard a voice saying unto him, Saul, Saul, why persecutest thou me? (5) And he said, Who art thou, Lord? And the Lord said, I am Jesus whom thou persecutest: it is hard for thee to kick against the pricks. (6) And he trembling and astonished said, Lord, what wilt thou have me to do? And the Lord said unto him, Arise, and go into the city, and it shall be told thee what thou must do.

You see Saul had a heart for God, but he didn't understand God's ways and was blinded by pride and misconception. It is very easy to fall into a mindset by the common opinion set forth by man's view of God. But we do not realize that God is far beyond the finite understanding of our minds. After this interaction between Jesus and Saul, there was deliverance on the road called Straight by a man called Ananias.

Act 9:8-18 KJV And Saul arose from the earth; and when his eyes were opened, he saw no man: but they led him by the hand, and brought him into Damascus. (9) And he was three days without sight, and neither did eat nor drink. (10) And there was a certain disciple at Damascus, named Ananias; and to him said the Lord in a vision, Ananias. And he said, Behold, I am here, Lord. (11) And the Lord said unto him, Arise, and go into the street which is called Straight, and enquire in the house of Judas for one called Saul, of Tarsus: for, behold, he prayeth, (12) And hath seen in a vision a man named Ananias coming in, and putting his hand on him, that he might receive his sight. (13) Then Ananias answered, Lord, I have heard by many of this man, how much evil he hath done to thy saints at Jerusalem: (14) And here he hath authority from the chief priests to bind all that call on thy name. (15) But the Lord said unto him, Go thy way: for he is a chosen vessel unto me, to bear my name before the Gentiles, and kings, and the children of Israel: (16) For I will shew him how great things he must suffer for my name's sake. (17) And Ananias went his way, and entered into the house; and putting his hands on him said, Brother Saul, the Lord, even Jesus, that appeared unto thee in the way as thou camest, hath sent me, that thou mightest receive thy sight, and be filled with the Holy Ghost. (18) And immediately there fell from his eyes as it had been scales: and he received sight forthwith, and arose, and was baptized.

Now Saul which is also Paul had become a believer and the Spirit of the Lord came into him and he began to see the truth as it really is concerning salvation. Paul was well educated in the scriptures and had the word of God in his heart so that he had a unique ability to teach the truth about Messiah Jesus from the scriptures. As he believed; he then could see and the more that he believed, the more that he could see. Paul had a heart that could be persuaded because he loved God more than man. Some of the Pharisees could not be convinced because of their intellectual position on faith. Pride is a locked door and keeps the truth from entering.

Joh 9:39-41 KJV And Jesus said, For judgment I am come into this world, that they which see not might see; and that they which see might be made blind. (40) And some of the Pharisees which were with him heard these words, and said unto him, Are we blind also? (41) Jesus said unto them, If ye were blind, ye should have no sin: but now ye say, We see; therefore your sin remaineth.

Can you see what Jesus is saying here? When you think that you already know something then you are not teachable. If you know that you could be wrong about something then you can hear the truth. Humility is the willingness to hear and consider what someone says to you and weigh it against the truth of God's word.

Pro 13:18 KJV Poverty and shame shall be to him that refuseth instruction: but he that regardeth reproof shall be honoured.

In Paul's case, it was tradition that caused him to fight against Christ because he thought that he knew better. But Paul after seeing Christ was humbled and became least in his own sight. Humility had caused him to see what he had been blinded to by pride. That is where the light comes in and illuminates the soul of a person. Fights break out because vanity and pride become more important than God's word. In Paul's life; the path that he was on was darkness even though he was a religious and pious man. The religion part is usually the thing that hinders your walk with Christ. Christianity is about knowing Jesus personally, but religion only knows about Him. You can learn all about God in the scriptures, but unless you are willing to ask Him into your heart and allow Him to lead you; then all you have is information. Look at the change in Paul; he went from destroying Christianity to giving his life to teach and defend it. Paul's conversion is one of great importance in that he shows us how God can change a person from the inside out. I am not the same person that I once was because God has changed me completely. I am no longer His enemy and I live my life for Him and not the old destructive ways. Paul has become a great light in God's pathway through this life as he has revealed the portrait of Christ that is in the Old Testament scriptures. The way of salvation is made clear and we by seeing Paul's conversion and life can find for ourselves that unique treasure that is only found in knowing Christ.

Jesus the Light of the world

As we look down the illuminated path, narrow in its scope, its direction can clearly be seen. At the end of it is a doorway; the only entrance whereby we may enter into the glory of God. This is the light that dispels the darkness and truly separates good from evil; this is the light of the world.

Luk 2:25-32 KJV And, behold, there was a man in Jerusalem, whose name was Simeon; and the same man was just and devout, waiting for the consolation of Israel: and the Holy Ghost was upon him. (26) And it was revealed unto him by the Holy Ghost, that he should not see death, before he had seen the Lord's Christ. (27) And he came by the Spirit into the temple: and when the parents brought in the child Jesus, to do for him after the custom of the law, (28) Then took he him up in his arms, and blessed God, and said, (29) Lord, now lettest thou thy servant depart in peace, according to thy word: (30) For mine eyes have seen thy salvation, (31) Which thou hast prepared before the face of all people; (32) A light to lighten the Gentiles, and the glory of thy people Israel.

All of the lights along that path carried with them the hope of glory and the light of life that is added to the eternal flame, that calls every person to enter where no one could before. Where there was darkness there is now light and where death reigned, now is life everlasting.

Early on in the beginning where the serpent had beguiled humanity to choose unwisely, the battle had begun. Their decision had allowed evil to enter in and mingle with good. Every light that we have seen throughout the corridors of history that light the path, have voluntarily chosen to turn their backs on evil. Evil was always present but they chose the good and became our guides that lead us to that glorious light that is Christ.

Isa 9:2 KJV The people that walked in darkness have seen a great light: they that dwell in the land of the shadow of death, upon them hath the light shined.

Jesus is the light of the world that has brought salvation to a lost and dying people. As Jesus walked upon the earth, He brought hope wherever He went. He healed the sick and caused the crippled to walk again. The blinded eyes were made to see and the deaf ears to hear again. Even the dead were raised again to life and the broken-hearted were given peace. Jesus gave His proof that He is the Son of God the Messiah.

Luk 4:16-21 KJV And he came to Nazareth, where he had been brought up: and, as his custom was, he went into the synagogue on the sabbath day, and stood up for to read. (17) And there was delivered unto him the book of the prophet Esaias. And when he had opened the book, he found the place where it was written, (18) The Spirit of the Lord is upon me, because he hath anointed me to preach the gospel to the poor; he hath sent me to heal the brokenhearted, to preach deliverance to the captives, and recovering of sight to the blind, to set at liberty them that are bruised, (19) To preach the acceptable year of the Lord. (20) And he closed the book, and he gave it again to the minister, and sat down. And the eyes of all them that were in the synagogue were fastened on him. (21) And he began to say unto them, This day is this scripture fulfilled in your ears.

These are blessed words because this scripture has prophesied of the Messiah that would come and save the world. The depression of hopelessness was upon us and there was no way out until He came with His light of glory to reveal the mercy and grace of the Almighty.

Joh 3:16-17 KJV For God so loved the world, that he gave his only begotten Son, that whosoever believeth in him should not perish, but have everlasting life. (17) For God sent not his Son into the world to condemn the world; but that the world through him might be saved.

We were once without hope in the world and dying the slow death of condemnation. The everlasting fires of the justice of God were our destination, and no one could escape. But there came a light down from Heaven and showed us the way to find peace. Knowing justice and because He is just, the penalty for our transgression had to be paid.

Heb 9:22 KJV And almost all things are by the law purged with blood; and without shedding of blood is no remission.

This is forever and a debt that had to be paid because God is just and perfect. No man could satisfy the enormous cost, so there had to be intervention by the hand of the only one that could. The spotless Lamb of God was prepared even before the world began. God could have stopped sin in the Garden of Eden and removed only two people and started over. But God is not bound by time and space as are we and He saw the end from the beginning. He looked out over the corridors of time and saw you and had compassion for you and loved you. He knew us before we were born; before our time had come. God is love and He; rather than to start over made a way to save us. There is no greater love than to sacrifice one's life for another. Jesus led all people to the cross of condemnation and there He sacrificed His own life on our behalf.

Luk 23:44-49 KJV And it was about the sixth hour, and there was a darkness over all the earth until the ninth hour. (45) And the sun was darkened, and the veil of the temple was rent in the midst. (46) And when Jesus had cried with a loud voice, he said, Father, into thy hands I commend my spirit: and having said thus, he gave up the ghost. (47) Now when the centurion saw what was done, he glorified God, saying, Certainly this was a righteous man. (48) And all the people that came together to that sight, beholding the things which were done, smote their breasts, and returned. (49) And all his acquaintance, and the women that followed him from Galilee, stood afar off, beholding these things.

The great light had been put out and darkness was all around and hope seemed to have deserted those that had trusted Him. A dark day indeed when the Light of the world was dead and darkness had replaced the void that He left behind. The sound of wailing brakes the silence of the moment and tears would water the ground and mingle with His spilled blood as His lifeless body hung between heaven and earth upon a rugged old cross. They had placed their hope in Messiah and now Messiah was dead and what good can He do now? However, they had forgotten the words that He spoke while He was alive.

Mat 16:21 KJV From that time forth began Jesus

to shew unto his disciples, how that he must go unto Jerusalem, and suffer many things of the elders and chief priests and scribes, and be killed, and be raised again the third day.

These words were the words from the tongue of the one that is called the truth. The hope that seemed to be lost was still an ember that was glowing and would in three days become ablaze once again. As the broken-hearted women approached the burial place, they would find their hope in the fascination of an empty tomb. The voice of hope would speak the words that will become a blaze of fire in the hearts of all that trusted in Christ.

*Luk 24:1-9 KJV Now upon the first day of the week, very early in the morning, they came unto the sepulchre, bringing the spices which they had prepared, and certain others with them. (2) And they found the stone rolled away from the sepulchre. (3) And they entered in, and found not the body of the Lord Jesus. (4) And it came to pass, as they were much perplexed thereabout, behold, two men stood by them in shining garments: (5) And as they were afraid, and bowed down their faces to the earth, they said unto them, **Why seek ye the living among the dead?** (6) He is not here, but is risen: remember how he spake unto you when he was yet in Galilee, (7) Saying, The Son of man must be delivered into the hands of sinful men, and be crucified, and the third day rise again. (8) And* *they remembered his words, (9) And returned from the sepulchre, and told all these things unto the eleven, and to all the rest.(emphasis added).*

Sin had been defeated once and for all; the cost had been paid and grace has replaced condemnation for all that believe. The great light is greater still and shines gloriously throughout eternity. All that come to this light are endowed by the same and now have become His hands and His feet and His voice for all the world to hear. Hope is restored and life has begun so the greatest of these lights that illuminate the path is leading the way into the very presence of God Himself.

The scriptures were given for us to learn and grow and become more than we were before. The invisible attributes of a person make them either ugly or beautiful. These attributes are the creation of choices in the life of a person as they decide the direction that they will take. God is a gentleman and will not Lord Himself over you to force you into His will. He has given the lights over history that we can follow on His path to life everlasting. While we are here inside of time and space, we can also become lights to dispel the darkness. Humility is the fuel for the greatness that can be attained as God is in the business of doing the impossible. Your life is very important to God and He can lift you high into the ranks of greatness, but you must humble yourself and give it back to Him. In God's hierarchy, the least shall be the greatest; servitude is the crowning achievement of those that become the greatest of all.